D!RTY®
SPANISH

D!RTY®
SPANISH

Everyday Slang from
"What's Up?" to "F*%# Off!"

SECOND EDITION

JUAN CABALLERO
illustrated by **LINDSAY MACK**

Ulysses Press

Published by:
Ulysses Press
P.O. Box 3440
Berkeley, CA 94703
www.ulyssespress.com

ISBN: 978-1-56975-923-3
Library of Congress Control Number: 2011925460

Printed in the United States by Bang Printing

20 19 18 17 16 15 14 13 12

Acquisitions editor: Nick Denton-Brown
Managing editor: Claire Chun
Project editor: Alice Riegert
Production: Abigail Reser
Spanish proofreader: Richard Harris
English proofreader: Lauren Harrison
Interior design: what!design @ whatweb.com
Cover design: Double R Design
Front cover photo: woman © FernandoAH/istockphoto.com
Back cover illustration: Lindsay Mack

Distributed by Publishers Group West

To my father, who taught me the lurid joys of profanity; to my mother, who taught me the inward satisfaction of pedagogy; and to you, dear reader, for paying me to combine the two.

TABLE OF CONTENTS

·····Acknowledgments

Juan wishes he had the space and recollection to thank everyone who helped him with this book, but circumstances conspire against it. Chapters and entire draft copies were reviewed by Caballeros María and Carlos, Victor Goldgel Carballo, Gabrielle Wolodarski, Ignacio Gatto Bellora, and Jorge Díaz-Velez. Roxana Fitch's website and the forum posters on wordreference.com also made this book possible, as did any number of anonymous wiki-ers, *piroperos*, smart-asses, graffiti artists, poets and criminals. And thanks to Francine Masiello for recommending me for the job with her habitual overconfidence in my abilities.

USING THIS BOOK

This book was written with the assumption that you already know enough Spanish to get by. After all, this is a slang book, and slang tends to be the last thing you learn after getting down all the basic (and relatively useless) sayings, like "I live in the red house" and "Yes, I like the library very much, thank you." This is a book designed to take your Spanish to the next level. So if you're looking for a grammar lesson, you're in the wrong spot. But if you want to tell your friend that he has a tiny dick or to get rid of the douchebag hitting on you in the bar, this is the book for you.

Every phrase in *Dirty Spanish* is up-to-date slang. Except in special cases, the English is given first, followed by the Spanish. Sometimes the Spanish is given with alternatives (*gordo/a, tu/s*) to account for gender or plural differences. This isn't a grammar book and you're not an idiot, so we expect that you'll be able to figure it out without any more explanation.

Unlike other volumes in the *Dirty* series, this book covers not *one* language but many. That's because Spanish is *not* universal. Colombian slang is quite different from Spanish or Mexican slang. Most of the slang included here, though, was chosen because it's easily understood in any Spanish-

PRONOUNCING SPANISH)))

Speaking Spanish like a *pinche gringo* will make you seem like, well, a *pinche gringo,* and will raise the price of everything you want to buy in proportion to how annoying your accent is. It can even mark you as an easy target for pickpockets or muggers. So get your pronunciation straight. You have three golden rules to remember:

1. *Watch your damn vowels* already! Each vowel is essentially the same in every context:

> A is always like the "a" in "father."
>
> O is always like the "o" in "bone."
>
> I is always like the "ie" in "wiener."
>
> E is always like the "e" in "wet."
>
> U is always like the "oo" in "poon," unless it comes after a "g" or a "q" and has no umlaut dots over it.

One of the biggest slipups that English speakers make when speaking Spanish is following the unconscious English pronunciation rules that make vowels change contextually, smuggling in foreign A's and turning every unstressed vowel into the "uuuuh" sound that Spanish speakers equate with the pronunciation of a village idiot (don't pruhtend you don't know whuht I'm talking uhbout).

2. *Pay attention to accents* when learning new words, and review the accent rules online or in your old grammar book before traveling. If you put the accent on the wrong syllable, people think you're saying another word, which, 99 percent of the time, is a word that doesn't exist. Americans are often shocked by not being understood for having fudged such a "minor" detail. But it's a major difference to Spanish speakers, so they, in turn, feel shocked when Americans walk around speaking gibberish and getting impatient with people.

3. *Don't overpronounce.* Pay attention to local pronunciation and try to keep up; it makes you sound natural and cool. Vowels and syllables sometimes drop out of the middle of long words (*no te pr'ocupas*). D's between vowels at the end of words often drop out to make a vowel diphthong (it's *complicao*). Consonants at the end of words in an unstressed syllable, particularly D's and S's, often get underpronounced or forgotten altogether (*de vera', no te procupah*).

In the Caribbean, this process is taken one step further, frequently coming right in the middle of a word (*¡Tú huele' com'u' pe'cao!*). Also, syllable emphasis can change from city to city, overriding the normal accent-placement of a word. Subtle slipups like mixing up the pronunciation between S and Z or T and D, however the word might actually be spelled, can mark you as foreign. So listen closely to how people pronounce words you thought you already knew.

speaking country. But there are many terms that are region- or country-specific. For all of those, we've included abbreviations in parenthesis for the region or country where the phrase comes from:

COUNTRY	ABBREVIATION
Latin America	LatAm
South America	S.Am
Central America	CenAm
Southern Cone (Argentina, Chile, and Uruguay)	S.Cone
Caribbean	Carib
Andes	Andes
México	Mex
Guatemala	Gua
El Salvador	ElS
Honduras	Hon
Nicaragua	Nic
Costa Rica	CoR
Panama	Pan
Cuba	Cub

Dominican Republic	DoR
Puerto Rico	PuR
Venezuela	Ven
Colombia	Col
Ecuador	Ecu
Peru	Per
Bolivia	Bol
Chile	Chi
Paraguay	Par
Uruguay	Uru
Argentina	Arg
Spain	Spn

Whenever a regional term is given in addition to a universal one, you can assume it'll sound more natural to someone from that region to hear that term. However, many regional words are rapidly becoming international as Latin American media culture continues to globalize, and as teenagers all over the world listen to MP3s and download TV shows from around the Spanish-speaking globe.

If personal curiosity or professional demands require you to know exactly where a given term is used, or if you want to dive deeper into the seedy world of Spanish slang, the easiest place to start is online:

www.rae.es—The Real Academia Española's online dictionary may not always be cutting-edge for Latin American slang, but at least it's reliable and accurate.

www.jergasdehablahispana.org—Roxana Fitch's invaluable, free, and searchable dictionary houses a massive collection of slang, sorted by region.

forum.wordreference.com — The Word Reference forums are a thriving international community of professional translators and amateur linguists where you can get answers from real people in the field.

The best language teacher, however, will always be immersion. So get to traveling, do some downloading, start YouTube-ing, or, at the very least, go to the Hispanic part of town and strike up some conversations — just don't start with the "Angry Spanish" chapter!

Now take your *Dirty Spanish* and get down and dirty with it!

CHAPTER 1

HOWDY SPANISH
QUÉ TAL-'STELLANO

Spanish speakers in a friendly (or alcoholic) environment rarely start conversations with an "*Hola*" or "*Buen día*." It's more casual and common to head straight for a question, even if it hangs in the air as hypothetical and unanswered (some people routinely answer *¿Qué tal?* with…*¿Qué tal?*).

•••••What's up?
¿Qué tal?

Many greetings, particularly short ones like *¿Qué dices?*, sound best followed by an affectionate, mildly offensive epithet (Tubby, Pizzaface, Nancy, Bigballs, whatever).

What's happenin'?
¿Qué pasó?
Only tourists and people over 30 use *qué pasa* in the present tense anymore.

What's up guys?
¿Qué hay de nuevo, muchachos?

What's goin' on?
¿Qué sapa?
Qué pasa in anagram form.

What're you up to?
¿Qué haces?

What's the good word, Tubby?
*¿**Qué dices**, Gordo?*

Whatcha got?
¿A ver?

What the cock have you been up to?
¿A verga?

What else is new with you?
De tu vida, ¿qué más?

What'd I miss?
¿Quihubo?

·····How you doing?
¿Cómo andas?

As in English, once you're done with the initial niceties and greetings, it's time to dig a little deeper and inquire about the person's life. Vague, fragmentary answers are the norm, so don't expect a lengthy response or even a complete sentence.

How are you?
¿Cómo estás?

How's it goin'?
¿Cómo te va? ; ¿Cómo le va?
To be chummy but still respectful, use the second one.

How you doin'?
¿Cómo andas? | ¿Cómo andamio? (S.Cone)

How's life?
¿Cómo anda la vida?

WHAT'S UP?)))
¿QUÉ TAL?

¿Qué tal-co? (S.Cone)

¿Qué tal andas? (Spn)

¿Qué jais? (Mex)

¿Qué volá? (Carib)

¿Qué más? (Andes)

¿Qué's la que hay? (PuR)

How's everything?
¿Cómo va todo?

How 'bout things with you?
¿Y tus cosas?

> **Kickin' ass!**
> *¡De pelos! | ¡A toda madre!* (Mex) *| ¡De butaca!* (S.Cone)

> **Straight chillin'.**
> *¡Todo tránqui'!*

> **I'm all right.**
> *Ando ahí nomás.*

> **It's all good!**
> *Todo [va] bien.*

> **Same as ever.**
> *Como siempre.*

> **Still putting around here, aren't I?**
> *Sigo por aquí, no? ; Aquí nomás.*

> **Everything's super.**
> *Todo a full. | ...full de to'.* (Carib)

> **Fine.**
> *En marcha.*

> **Never better.**
> *Nunca mejor.*

> **Great.**
> *A todo dar.* (LatAm)

Super.
De órdago. (Spn)

Peachy.
Bola. (Spn)

Awesome.
Increíble.

I can't complain.
No me quejo.

It's whatever. (meaning, it is what it is.)
Es lo que sea.

It's whatever. (meaning, I feel whatever about it.)
Me da lo mismo.

Shitty.
Una cagada.

Fucking crappy.
Como el orto. (S.Am)

Fucked up.
Jodido.

I'm in a bad fucking mood.
Vengo encabronado.
Estoy encabronado would be more literal, but *vengo* is kind of a warning to the listener that the bad mood's been on for a while…

·····How's life, really?
¿Pero en serio, cómo te va la vida?

Even if your friend didn't mention any girl/boy/work/family troubles last time you talked, it's fair game to ask them about it point-blank if you've heard things through the grapevine.

What's the dilly with…?
¿Qué onda con…?

What's the latest with…?
¿Qué cuentas sobre…? ; ¿Qué se cuenta de…?

  your old lady
  la vieja

the ball-n-chain
la jefa ; la domadora

your folks
los viejos | los tatas (Mex)

The whole situation is seriously fucked.
*Todo el asunto está **seriamente jodido**.*

I don't even wanna talk about it.
Ni hablar.

What's happenin' with that little venture?
*¿Que pasó con ese **bisnes**?*

> **It's scraping by.**
> ***En algo** está.*

How's your chump job?
*¿Qué pasó con el **curro**?* (Spn) | *...la **chamba**?* (Mex) |
*...la **changa**?* (S.Cone) | *...el **camello**?* (Andes)

> **Gettin' paid**, at least.
> ***Me pagan**, por lo menos.*

> **They're really wiping their asses with me.**
> *Me están **pasando por el culo**.*

·····Clueless
Despistado

I dunno...
No sé...

> **I don't know what to tell you.**
> *No sabría qué decirte.*

> **I have no clue.**
> *No tengo ni idea.*

[I have] not the slightest idea.
Ni la más pálida idea [tengo].

I have no fucking idea.
Ni puta idea.

Shit if I know.
¿Qué se yo?

How the fuck would I know?
¿Y yo, qué mierda sé? | *…qué coño…* (Spn, Carib) |
…qué cojones… (Mex)

God only knows.
Sepa el Señor.

Who knows?
Sepa Fulano. | *…Pancha.* (Mex) | *…Moya.* (Chi)
Literally, "Random dude knows."

Fucked if I know.
¡Sepa la bola! | *…la chingada!* (Mex)

·····Look who showed up!
¡Mira quién apareció!

It's common among good friends to express exaggerated
surprise or joy at an arrival, particularly a late one. These
expressions seem dramatic in English, but are a normal part
of interacting in Spanish-speaking lands. It's common in these
situations to call someone by a nickname that would, in other
contexts, be way more offensive, like *pendejo de mierda* (total
fucker) or *hijo de la gran puta* (son of a royal whore).

Long time no see!
¡Tanto tiempo!

You made it, Dopey!
¡Caíste, salame! (S.Cone)

They let you out!
¡Te dejaron salir!

Here he is, back from the dead!
¡Uppaa, llegó el desaparecido!
Be careful with this one in the Southern Cone, where *los
desaparecidos* refers to people who "disappeared" during
various murder-happy dictatorships.

Speak of the devil…and he doth appear.
Hablando del Rey de Roma…por la puerta asoma. ;
…el burro se asoma.

What the heck are you doing here?
¿Y tú, qué haces por aquí?

Great to see you!
¡Qué alegría verte!

You look great!
¡Qué pinta!

Where've you been hidin'?
¿Dónde te has metido?

You fell off the face of the earth.
Te esfumaste de la faz de la Tierra.

You've put on a few [pounds] since the last time I saw you, Tubby!
Te engordaste un par [de kilos], ¡Rechonchito!

Just when we were too few, and then…
¡Tras que éramos pocos, y…

> **Granny** gave birth!
> *parió la abuela!*
> Don't ask me why this perverse spectacle would make for
> a kick-ass party…but it is definitely a common saying!

> **my brother hired a drag queen!**
> *mi hermano trajo un travestí!*

> **the wild beast / the deaf girl / so-and-so**
> **showed up!**
> *llegó la bestia / la sorda / fulano!*

> **Doofus** showed up!
> *cayó el tronco!*

·····Hey!
¡Oye!

At some point, you'll probably need to catch someone's attention in a crowded street, open-air market, barfight, or orgy. There are a bunch of ways to do so, but most are pretty regional—there's no universal "hey" aside from *oye* (listen) and *mira* (look), and even those have regional connotations (like in Argentina, where they sound more confrontational, like "listen up!").

Hey!
¡*Oye!* | ¡*Aguas!* (Mex) | ¡*Mare!* (Mex) | ¡*Ala!* (Andes) | ¡*Che!* (S.Cone)
Che is a trademark of the Argentine dialect, where it means both "hey" and "guy." Borges once "Argentinized" the story of Caesar and Brutus by substituting the famous "*et tu, Brutus*?" with an angry "¡*Pero, che!*"

Hey, man!
¡*Quetá, compa!*

Hey, now!
¡*Épale!*

Watch out! / Eeeasy there.
¡*Eeeeeeh-pa!*

WOW!)))
¡CARAMBA!

If you want to sound like a hokey Ned Flanders anywhere you are in the Spanish-speaking world, then go ahead and use *caramba*. If not, here are some regional-specific alternatives.

¡*Fua!* (S.Cone) | ¡*Úchale!* (Mex) | ¡*Diay!* (CenAm) | ¡*Caray!* (Andes) | ¡*Gua!* (Spanglish) | ¡*Hala!* (Spn)

Look!
¡Mira!

Listen!
¡Oye!

Listen up, deaf guy!
¡Oye, sordo! | *¡Oye, teniente!* (Spn)

Wake up, space-cadet!
¡Oye, ausente! ; ¡Oye, zombi!

No way!
¡No me digas!

Jesus Christ!
¡Cristo mío!

Holy shit!
¡Dio[s] mío!

I can't believe it!
¡No lo puedo creer!

Really?
¿De veras?

For real?
¿En serio?

Give it to me straight.
¡Dime la dura! | *…la firme!* (Peru) | *…la posta!* (S.Cone) | *…la fetén!* (Spn) | *…la neta!* (CenAm)

Yeah?
¿Sí?

You think?
¿Te parece?

Na-ah.
Ni modo.

Hell yeah!
¡Del todo!

That's fucked up!
¡Qué mierda!

Check this out!
¡Chéquele! | *¡Chécate esto!* (Mex)

Check out that hairy guy's **back-bush!**
¡Cheque la barba dorsal que tiene ese gorila!*

·····Goodbye
Adiós

For some reason, Spanish farewells are a blank check for corniness. *Ciao*, the most common slang for "good-bye," is sometimes spelled phonetically, so don't be baffled by a *chau* or a *chao* on a billboard or in a comic book. *Ciao* is so common that many Latin Americans would be surprised if you told them it's actually Italian.

Later!
¡Ciao!

Lates!
¡Chabela! ; ¡Chavela!
From *Ciao, bella.*

In a while, crocodile.
Chaufa. (Per)
This is a horrible Peruvian pun on Chinese food: *ciaofun.*

Bye y'all. (hick, countryish way of saying "bye")
Chado. (Andes)

See ya around!
¡Ahí nos vemos!

See ya in a bit!
¡Ahí nos vidrios!

Let's roll.
Larguémonos.

Let's get outta here.
Ahuécamos el ala.

I'm outie.
Me marcho.

I'm off.
Salgo rajando.

I'm leaving.
Me voy.

I'm gone.
Me fui.

I gotta bounce.
Tengo que huir.

Text me!
¡Mensajéame! ; ¡Textéame!

Call me later!
¡Llámame luego!

Toodles!
¡Ahí nos Belmont! (Chi)

We're outta here.
Nosotros nos huimos.

See ya later!
¡Hasta luego!

L8R.
Elejota.
The phonetic pronunciation of *L.J.*, which is the abbreviation for *los juimos*, Chilean slang for "Let's go."

Until next time!
¡Hasta la próxima!

Smell ya later!
¡Hasta el cante! (Spn) | *¡Hasta el hornazo!* (Mex) | *¡Hasta la chucha!* (Andes) | *¡Hasta la baranda!* (S.Cone)

·····Blessings and graces
Bendiciones y gracias

Catholicism is as widespread in Spain and Latin America as advertising is in America or drinking is in Ireland. And just as the British will say "Cheers" as you hand them an Alcoholics Anonymous pamphlet, many Spanish speakers will literally bless you even if you're wearing a yarmulke and a giant star of David.

May God go with you.
Que vaya Dios contigo.

Fare thee well.
Que le vaya bien.

May God watch over you.
Que Dios te guarde.

May things go swell for you.
Que te vaya bonito.

If God so wills, no more freeways will collapse.
Si Dios quiere, no se derrumbarán más autopistas.

God and the new budget willing, we'll get a raise on the 4th.
Mediante Dios y el presupuesto nuevo, nos dan un aumento de sueldo el día 4.

I pray to God that my car won't fail me again.
Ojalá que no me falle el coche de nuevo.

·····Sorry
Sori

In Spanish, you don't so much apologize as plead distraction, momentary lapse of reason, ill luck, or simply general incompetence. Most Spanish speakers use self-deprecation to extract themselves from a sticky situation rather than beg forgiveness. So if you get caught cheating on your girlfriend or boyfriend, just say, "Whoops, aren't I the sillyhead!" and then grin until your cheeks hurt.

Sorry!
¡Perdón! ; ¡Sorri! ; ¡Sori!

I'm really, really sorry!
¡Lo siento muchísimo!

My bad.
Emece.
As in "M.C.": mea culpa

Well excuuuuse me.
Cien mil disculpas, señor mío.

Ooops!
¡Ufa!

It's totally my fault.
Tengo todo la culpa.

My deepest apologies!
¡Mil disculpas!

I went too far.
Se me fue la mano.

I crossed the line.
Me pasé de la raya.

Forgive me.
Perdóname.

I'm so embarrassed!
¡Qué vergüenza! | ¡Qué corte! (Spn)

I'm so humiliated!
¡Qué pena me da!

I'm such an idiot!
¡Qué idiota soy!

What a stupid thing to do!
¡Qué idiotez! ; ¡Qué huevada!

What a fuck-up!
¡Qué cagazón! (Mex) | ¡Qué boludez! (S.Cone)

·····Get over it
Aguántatelo

If apologizing doesn't get you off the hook, you should move for a full dismissal of charges. Some people just won't listen to reason and need to be told to shut the hell up and stop acting like a little bitch.

Let's not get carried away.
No es para tanto.

It's not what it looks like!
¡No es lo que parece!

I didn't mean to.
Fue sin querer.

I didn't mean to shit in your bidet!
*¡Cagué en tu **bidet** sin querer!*

Oh, don't make a scene!
*¡Ay, no **armes un escándolo**! | ¡Deja el show!* (Pur)

Take it easy.
Tómalo con calma. | Cógelo suave. (Carib)

Chill out, man, it's just a dribble of urine.
*Calma, hombre, es **un chorrito** de orina **nomás**.*

·····'Scuse me
'Miso

Latins don't have many ways of saying "excuse me." As the old saying goes, *Mejor pedir perdón que pedir permiso* (Better to apologize later than ask permission beforehand).

Excuse me.
Con permiso.

'Scuse me.
Permiso.

HELP A BROTHER OUT)))
ÉCHAME UN CABLE, 'MANO

Be a pal.	*Sé buen amigo.*
Be a buddy.	*Sé valedor.* [Mex]
Be a team player.	*Sé jalador.* [Mex]
Be a stand-up dude.	*Sé paleta.* [Chi]
Be a real chum.	*Sé tronco.*

Meepmeep.
'Miso-miso.

Make way, I'm in a rush.
Abre paso, *vengo apurado.*

Watch out!
¡Cuidado!

Back in a flash!
¡Vuelvo rapidingo!

·····Please
Porfa

Spanish slang is supertheatrical—you'll often see adults
pleading like children for a simple favor. That's because
you don't merely ask someone for something; you paint them
as your supreme benefactor, a noble gaucho and angelic do-
gooder who would forever be immortalized in song if they
could somehow bring it upon themselves to pass the goddamn salt.

Pleeeeease!
¡Poorfaa!

Pretty please!
¡Plis-plis!

Please do me the favor.
*Por favor, hágame **el favor**. | ...**la gauchada**.* (S.Cone) |
*...**la volada**.* (CenAm) | *...**el cruce**.* (Col)

I'm beggin you!
¡Te lo ruego!

You scratch my back and I'll scratch yours.
¡Hazme un cambalache!

Please have the decency to shut that gossiping
mouth of yours.
Tenga la bondad *de callar esa boca chismosa, por favor.*

¡INTRODUCING YOURSELF)))

My name is Ingelbert.
Me llamo Ingelberto.

I'm from Germany.
Vengo de Alemania.

I'm six-foot-four and hung like a donkey.
Mido dos metros y traigo un bulto como un burro.

They call me the Princess.
Me llaman la Princesa.

I'm Canadian. It's like an American, except without a gun.
Soy canadiense. Es como un yanqui, pero sin arma.

But I can still snap you like a twig, so stay where you are.
Igual puedo romperte como una paja, entonces quédate ahí.

Help me out!
¡Échame una mano!

Can you do me a favor?
¿Me harías una cosita?

·····Good to meet ya
Un placer darte a conocer

After meeting someone, it's always nice to express your pleasure at having done so. People like to be liked. Go figure.

Pleased to meet you.
Mucho gusto.

Please-ta meetcha.
'Chogusto.

I'm charmed.
Encantado.

The pleasure is all mine.
El placer es todo mío.

Likewise.
Igualmente.

It was nice to finally meet you.
Por fin tengo el placer de conocerte.

Have a good one.
Que le vaya bien.

Hopefully, we'll bump into each other again.
*A ver si **nos encontramos** por ahí.*

·····What do you do for fun?
¿Cómo te diviertes?

Once you've established that someone's gonna be at your table for a while and you've exhausted all the small talk, it's far more acceptable than in the U.S. to press for personal details.

What do you do to kill the time?
¿Cómo matas las horas?

Where are your people from?
*¿De dónde viene **tu gente**?*

How long have you lived in the city?
¿Desde cuándo has vivido en la ciudad?

Where were you raised?
¿Dónde te criaste?

Can you show me around the city?
¿Me podrías pasear por la ciudad?

I don't know anyone here, can I sit with you?
No conozco/a un alma aquí, ¿podría sentarme contigo?

Let's hang out later tonight.
Nos juntamos a la tarde, ¿que te parece?

How single are you, exactly?
*¿**Cuán soltero** estás, de hecho?*

WHEN iN ROME...DON'T CALL THEM ROMANS)))

Know how people in New York like to call themselves New Yorkers and say they live in the Big Apple? Well, they stole that habit from Spanish speakers just like they stole Manhattan from the Indians. Here's a handy chart of the affectionate names Spanish speakers call themselves and their cities.

People who live in:	Call themselves:	And their city:
Buenos Aires	Porteños	Baires, Buesas
Madrid	Madrileños, Gatos	El Foro
Barcelona	Barceloneses, Barcelona	Barna, Barça
Mexico City	Chilangos	El Monstruo
Guadalajara	Tapatios	Guanatas
Lima	Limeños, Zapallos	
Guatemala City	Chapines	
El Salvador	Guanacos	
Nicaragua	Nicas	
Costa Rica	Ticos	

Where'd you learn **to open bottles** like that?
*¿Dónde aprendiste **a descorchar botellas** así?*

Would you give me **a private lesson**?
*¿Me darías **una lección privada**?*

What team do you play for, if you don't mind my asking?
*¿**Para qué equipo juegas**, si no te molesta la pregunta?*

CHAPTER 2

FRIENDLY SPANISH
CASTELLANO AMISTOSO

The best way to internalize the rhythms of Spanish-speaking society is to watch *telenovelas* for a few hours a day and read some smutty comics. These pulpy media are a great way to sharpen your verbal and judgmental skills on fictional victims.

•••••Real friends
Amigotes

Spanish speakers have tons of words to describe their range of friends, many based on degrees of closeness. Even more so than usual, these terms vary not only from country to country, but also within countries, between classes, between cities, or even by neighborhood or social circle.

Best-bud
Amigote/a

> **He's my best friend from back in the day.**
> *Es mi **amigote** desde hace mucho.* | ...**pana**...(Carib)

Homie
Compinche | *Asere* (Carib)

BFF
Cuate (CenAm)

Homeboy
Esse (Spanglish)

Old school chum
El/La cole (short for *colega*)

> **I miss my old school friends.**
> *Extraño a mis **coles**.*

Roommate (flatmate)
Compañero de departmento

Roommate (share a bedroom)
Compañero de habitación

Roommate (stranger from Craigslist)
Coinquilino

A girl (youngish)
Una nenita

> **Who's that little girl?**
> *Esa **nenita**, ¿quién es?*

Some random dude
Un tipo cualquiera | Un tío cualquiera (Spn)

> **She hooked up with some random dude last night.**
> *Ella se enrolló con **un tipo cualquiera** anoche.*

Punk kid
Chamaco/a (Mex) | *Pibe/a* (S.Cone) | *Chaval/a* (Spn)

> **Don't get huffy, he's just a punk kid.**
> *No te encabrones, es un **chamaco** nomás.*

A chick
Una chava | Una mina (S.Cone)

> **Your sister's a cool chick.**
> *Tu hermana es **buena chava**.*

A bastard
Un cabrón/ona (Mex)

> **Your brother's a real bastard.**
> *Tu hermano es **un cabronazo**.*

My bro
Mi 'mano | Mi carnal (Mex)

> **How you been, bro?**
> *¿Cómo viene la cosa, **'mano**?*

My sis
Mi 'mana

> **What's new, sis?**
> *¿Qué hay de nuevo, **'mana**?*

My boy
Mi compa' | Mi compai

> **We've been boys forever.**
> *Somos **compas** desde siempre.*

My girl
Mi comay

> **Don't worry about her; she's my girl.**
> *No te preocupes por ella—es **mi comay**.*

Drinking buddy
Compañebrio
Compañero (comrade) plus *ebrio* (drunk).

Dogg
Chavo (Mex)

Brah
Mijo/a
Although this is a term of endearment mothers use for their children, it can also be used as an affectionate, or more commonly, sarcastically affectionate, form of address between friends.

The guys
Los muchachos

> **He's fooling around with the guys.**
> *El está al pedo con **los muchachos**.*

Peeps
Mi gente

Crew
La clica | *El corillo* (Carib)
Clica comes from the French *clique*. It means "gang," as in "the gang," or the more serious "nowadays he's in a gang."

Posse
Aleros (CenAm)
Literally, "wingmen."

Bosom buddies
Amigos del alma

> **They've been bosom buddies since they were little.**
> *Han sido **amigos del alma** desde chicos.*

My confidant
Mi tumba
This derives from the old saying "Take it to your tomb."

> **I only tell you this 'cuz you're my confidant, understand?**
> *Contártelo a ti es contárselo a **mi tumba**, ¿entiendes?*

Good people
Buena gente

> **You can trust Jaime, he's good people.**
> *Puedes confiar en Jaime, es **buena gente**.*

•••••Duuuuuuude
Chavóoooon

As in any language, there are some names you say and others you just yell drunkenly across the bar at the end of the night. Here are the more affectionate ways to holler at your dude-bros.

Man!
¡Macho!

Dude!
¡Chavo!

Duuuuuuude!
¡Chavóoooon!

That guy
El tipo ese

Acquaintance
Conocido/a

Babe
Una buenota | Un pibón (Spn)

Who's that broad you came with?
*Y **esa tipa** con quien llegaste, ¿quién es?*

Chicky!
¡Chava!

Sweetheart!
¡Queriiido! (Arg)
This literally means "beloved," but somehow, even the manliest working-class Argies call each other this with no homoerotic connotation whatsoever.

·····Moms and pops
Mami y tata

Everyone's got a mother and a father. Unless you're an orphan, were born to gay parents, or were painfully abandoned as a child—in which case you can pretend your therapist is your *madre de leche*.

Daddy
Papi | Pai (Carib) | *Papay* (Andes)
In the mouth of an adult, *papi* usually has the same nasty connotation that "daddy" would have in English, as in "Oooh, Daddy, don't stop!"

Dad
Papá | Apá (Mex)

Pops
El tata (LatAm) | *El taita* (Carib, Andes)

My old man / My old lady
Mi viejo / Mi vieja

A bad father
El pudre
This pun on *padre* literally means, "He rots."

Doofus dad
El tato
Tato literally connotes a stutterer with a hard-T speech impediment.

Mommy
Mamá | Amá (Mex) | *Mamay* (Andes)

Moms
Mami | Mai (Carib)

Stepmother (wicked or otherwise)
La madrastra
The suffix *-astra* means "secondary" (and implies "wicked") in many other family terms: *padrastro, abuelastra, hermanastro…*

DOUBLE MEANINGS)))
DOBLE-SENTIDOS

After you've been speaking Spanish for a while, you'll start to notice how a lot of it can be taken as innocent dialogue or as sexually charged innuendo.

> Please-ta meetcha, what was it again?
> *Chogusto, ¿cómo era?*
>
> It's Paco, and the **deep pleasure** has been all mine, **Linda (Beautiful)**.
> *Es Paco, y el **placer hondo** ha sido todo mío, Linda.*
>
> But my name is Anna.
> *Pero yo me llamo Anna.*
>
> A fact of which I am deeply aware.
> *Ya lo sé a fondo.*
>
> Are you **pulling my leg**?
> *¿Me estás **cachondeando**?*
> *Cachondeando* is a versatile word that refers to bullshitting, flirting, and when a dog humps your leg.
>
> Nothing of the sort, my lady; on the contrary, I am entirely **at your disposal**.
> *Nada de eso, mi reina; yo estoy, todo lo contrario, entéramente **a tus órdenes**.*
>
> Well, if you are "entirely," maybe I'll have some **gruntwork** for you one of these days.
> *Bueno, si lo eres "enteramente," acaso tenga alguna **faena** para ti un día de estos.*

Mother figure / adoptive mother
Madre de leche

You got momma's-boy-itis.
Tienes la mamitis.

Your mom!
¡La madre que te parió!

You talkin' about my mom?
¿Estás mentando a mi madre?

·····Other fam
Otros en la fami

Most nicknames for family members are pretty regional, but here are the universal basics.

Get out the rocker for Gramps.
*Traiga la mecedora para **el abue'**.* | *...**el yayo**.* (Spn) |
*...**el nono**.* (S.Cone, from the Italian)

Your gramma is still kinda hot.
*Tu **abue'** sigue medio buena.* | *...**yaya**...* (Spn) |
*...**nona**...* (S.Cone)

Easy there, old-timer.
*Con calma, **anciano/a**.* | *...**ruco/a**.* (Mex)

You better get married quick if you don't want an illegitimate son.
*Tienes que casarte pronto si no quieres un **hijo natural**.*

The title of my honors thesis is "Fatherless Sons: The Legacy of Colonialism."
*El título de mi tesis de honores es "**Hijos espurios**: legados del colonialismo."*

Fidel Castro was the bastard son of a sugar planter.
*Fidel Castro fue el **hijo bastardo** de un hacendado de azúcar.* | *...**guacho**...* (S.Cone)

He thinks he's the head of the household, but his wife brings home the bacon.
*Él se piensa **padre de familia**, pero la esposa trae la lana.*

Man, your wife plays the housewife, but she couldn't bake you a *tres leches* to save her life.
*Ufa, tu mujer se viste bien de **madre de familia**, pero ni soñar que te haga un tres leches como la gente.*

That boy's one apple that didn't fall far from the tree.
*Ese chico **sí que salió hijo de su padre/madre**.*

·····Booty calls
Consuelos sexuales

Most Spanish speakers don't think of sexual adventures as immoral or depraved unless they're jealous old schoolmarms addicted to *telenovelas*. And even then there's something tongue-in-cheek about their aspersions. These handy names for all the shades of gray between singledom and married life are less judgmental than their English equivalents. Don't be shocked to hear them used between people who don't know each other very well.

I gotta find me a…
Necesito encontrarme un/una…

boyfriend. / girlfriend.
novio. / novia.

live-in girlfriend.
arrejuntada. | *juntada.* (CenAm)

lover.
amante.
Amante doesn't always imply sex, just intensity—so don't panic if someone says your 10-year-old sister has a lover!

companion. / partner. (domestic)
'ñera. / 'ñero.

friend with benefits.
amigovio/a. | *el/la jeva.* (Carib)
Amigo + novio = amigovio.

little somethin' on the side.
segundo frente.

fuckbuddy.
tragón/a.
This awesome word literally means "expert swallower" or "gulper." With a name like that, who *wouldn't* want a fuckbuddy?

booty call.
consuelo sexual.

Sounds like you need to make a booty call.
*Suena como que necesitas **hacerte una llamada
caliente**.*

It's too early for that, we're still in second gear.
*Es temprano para eso, todavía estamos en **grado dos**. ;
…en **segunda**.*

You guys aren't even shacking up yet?
*¿Ustedes ni siquiera **se** han **arrejuntado**?*

•••••Office dynamics
Dinámica de oficina

Real life is just like *The Office*, except sad and not funny.
Like most people, you probably hate your job because you're
surrounded by incompetent assholes, brown-nosing suck-
ups, and shitty coworkers with almost as many annoying
personal habits as the number of hours of your life you've
wasted in their company. Here are some ways for you to
defame all those no-talent clowns behind their backs.

Coworker
Colega ; Compañero/a

Boss
Jefe

Overlord/slave driver
Patron/a

I share my cubicle with a real **suck-up**.
*Comparto mi cubículo con un **lambiscón/a** total. ;
…**lambón**…*

What an **ass-kisser!**
*¡Qué **lameculos**! | ¡Qué **chupaculos**! (S.Cone)*

You gotta be a **yes-man** to get ahead.
*Tienes que ser un **pelotillero/a** para sobresalir.*

That **Goody Two-shoes** never calls in sick.
*Ese **beato/a** nunca se reporta enfermo/a.*

Just don't let **Mr. Overtime** get involved. (no talent,
buckets of extra effort)
*No dejes que se meta **el Empollón**.*
In school or research-oriented professions like law, you can also
use the more vivid *tragalibros*.

Watch out, here comes the **whip cracker**.
*Ojo, que viene el **tirante**. | …el **bretel**. (S.Cone)*

Don't leave the decision up to that **waffler**.
*No dejes la decisión al **panqueque** ese.*

An opportunist like her is always waiting to **stab you
in the back**.
***Una veleta** como ella siempre está dispuesta a darte **la
puñalada trapera**.*
Una veleta means "weather vane," as in, faces wherever the
wind's blowing.

I gotta pull the deadweight of my **slacker** coworkers.
*Estoy condenado al remo por los **desganados** de mis
colegas.*

I'm a **do-nothing** and I do it well.
*Soy un **quedado** y me quedo muy bien.* |
*...un **queso**...* (S.Cone)

He would be a doorman if he **weren't the boss's nephew.**
*Sería el portero si **no tuviera el padre alcalde**.*

You sure love **to brown-nose** him, don'tcha?
*¿Gozas mucho de **chuparle las medias**, o no?* |
*...**hacerle la pelota**...* (Spn)

•••••Life of the party
El vacilón

Every great party I've ever been to has had some awesome guy in a bizarro costume jumping on the couch and spraying Jaeger across the room like he just won the World Series. Unfortunately, I've been to just as many lame-ass parties populated by moochers, buzzkills, and straight-up nerds, the type of puritanical nancies who suddenly get too tired to play any more strip poker on the same hand they lose their pants. So quit acting like a *pinchaglobos*, grab the Don Julio, and *quítate los pantalones* already!

You are a/the...!
¡Eres un/una...!

He/She is (a)...
¡Él/Ella es (un/una)...!

What a...!
¡Qué...!

Quit being so/such a...!
¡No seas tan/un/una...!

life of the party
vacilón/ona

party animal
calavera

party pooper
aguafiestas

buzzkill
cortamambos

wet blanket
pinchaglobos

freeloader
aprovechado | *piola* (S.Cone)

moocher
remo
A *remo* is an oar—something that never pulls its own weight.

professional crasher
paracaidista

social butterfly / quick friend
amiguero/a (LatAm) | *macanudo/a* (S.Cone)
Outside the Southern Cone, *macanudo* just means
"upstanding" or "morally good."

out of it, in one's own world
ensimismado/a

phoney
plástico/a

sheltered nerd
nerdo | *zanahoria* (Andes) | *estafón* (PuR) |
zapallo (S.Cone)

boring / wearisome
pesado/a | *pelma* (Spn)

conversational zero
lastre ("ballast") ; *plomazo* ("lead") ; *una plasta* ("blob")

Valium on legs
soporífico/a ("a sedative") ; *un/a bajanota*

show-off
fanfarrón/ona | *echón* (PuR)

real talker
picudo/a (Mex)

·····Class
Cuna

Americans are sometimes shocked at how openly people in other countries talk about class. And class-talk is super common in Latin America and Spain, where there existed an honored aristocracy until quite recently (in many areas, the last names of the moneyed class still haven't changed). So don't be surprised when casual conversation takes a sudden turn for the socioeconomic.

He/She is so…
Él/Ella es tan…

uppity.
afectado/a.

pretentious.
agrandado/a. | *pituco/a.* (S.Cone, Andes)

fake.
plástico/a.

common.
ordinario/a.

tacky.
cursi.

trashy.
jarca.

stingy.
codo.
Literally, "elbow," as in, willing to put in a lot of elbow grease to save a drink.

chi-chi.
paquete.

blue-blooded.
de alcurnia. | *de cuna.* (S.Cone)

working-class.
de plebea.

top-notch.
de categoría. | *de catego.* (Mex)

TAKING THEM DOWN A NOTCH)))
BAJÁNDOLES LOS HUMOS

Stuck up	*Fufurufo/a*
Ned Flanders	*Santurrón/Santurrona*
Gullible	*Ñoño/a*
Lowlife	*Canalla*
Laughingstock	*Un/una hazmerreír*
Ex-con [lit. or fig.]	*Reo/a*
Crass	*Grosero/a*
Brat	*Un/una niñato/a*
Bossy	*Mandón/Mandona*
A curmudgeon	*Un/una infeliz*
Pussy-whipped	*Un "siquerida"* (a "Yes, dear!")
Hermit	*Padre del yermo*
A decrepit old geezer	*Un vejestorio decrépito*

He's a total poseur.
Con él, todo es pura pose.

How did that hoochie manage to marry a doctor?
¿Cómo llegó a casarse con un doctor esa guarra?

She wishes she was an A-list celebrity.
Ella sueña con ser una de la farándula.

All those fashion designers in Mexico City are just wannabe Euros.
Todos esos diseñadores de moda chilangos son unos europizantes. | ...unos malinchistas. (Mex)
Everyone in Mexico considers Mexico City to be full of Eurocentric, wannabe sellouts—kinda like how Texans think of New York City.

I like girls from good homes.
Por mi parte, yo prefiero a las niñas bien.

·····Characters
Personajes

As in any language, there are certain terms that are used less to describe than to designate or typify. Every social circle (and every *telenovela*, at least by the second season) has at least one good specimen of each of the following:

Gossip
Chismoso/a

Snoop
Entremetido/a | *Metiche* (LatAm)
Meter means "to get into," as in, other people's business.

Small-town boy
Pueblerino/a

Hick
Paleto/a

Hippie
Hippy
Uninflected whether for men or women, plural or singular, noun or adjective—occasionally spelled *jipi*, but usually spelled the English way.

Good-for-nothing
Inútil

Slacker
Huevón/ona

Bum
Vago

Badass
Gallito | *Chingón* (Mex)

Thug
Bruto

POLiTiCALLY iNCORR@CT)))
POLÍTICAMENTE INCORRECTO

Mexicanear
In a prison or criminal context, to snatch the heist from another thief or group of thieves; figuratively, to steal someone else's boyfriend or girlfriend right out from under them.

Hacer la uruguaya
A sleight-of-hand (or of tongue) at the cash register intended to get you more change than you're owed.

Gitanear
To smooth-talk, butter up, or scam. Also, to "gyp" someone... oh wait.

Peruanear
To shoot the shit, kill time, slack off, or goof off. In Southern Cone, also used as a synonym for *gitanear*.

Argentinear
To talk loudly and say nothing; to make an exuberant display of false erudition or plagiarized ideas.

Trabajar como un chino
It wasn't just in California that nineteenth century Cantonese-speaking immigrants built the railroads and laundered the shirts—most of the Hispanic world got at least a few thousand able-bodied newcomers during those years and proceeded to give them the worst work they could find.

No hay moros en la costa
The coast is clear! This phrase dates back to Spain's religious wars to push the Catholic–Muslim boundary to Gibraltar, even though nowadays *moro* can refer to people of recent as well distant African or Arab descent, depending on the context.

Dork
Nerd | Nerdo | Capullo (Spn)

Geek
Freaky
Sometimes spelled phonetically: *friqui*.

Fuck-up
Pato criollo (S.Cone) | *Gilipolas* (Spn)

Slut
Culisuelta
Literally, "Loose ass!"

Playboy
Mujeriego
This can also mean a "ladies' man" for you *machistas* out there.

Those two are total whores.
Ellas son un par de cueros totales.

Social climber
Un/una trepa
Literally, "climbs."

·····The gays
Los gay

Despite the "macho" reputation, the Hispanic world has plenty of queers, and gay tourism is booming (with tons of bearded dudes, beaches galore, and never-ending parades of slushy drinks sipped out of fruit husks, it's just like San Francisco, but warmer). Spanish speakers neutralize gay-bashing terms by using them affectionately, calling one another "Faggy" (*Marica*), for instance, just as they call each other "Fatty" (*Gordito*). But the interpretation is all in your tone, so make sure you use the following words like a sweetly cooing trannybar hostess and not like some degenerate skinhead.

Since when does he/she dress like a...?
¿Desde cuándo se viste él/ella como...?

faggot
un maricón | *un joto* (Mex)

fag / faggy
un marica
If you hear *marica* bandied about in Colombia, don't freak out. Colombians use this word liberally to mean "buddy" or "pal."

nancy
una mariposa
Literally, "a butterfly."

queen
un mariposo ; una loca

twink
una mariquita

femme
un/una hembra

butch
una macho | *una machona* (Andes, S.Cone) | *una machorra* (Mex)

bulldyke
una marimacha ; una machúa

lesbo
una tortillera (Mex) | *una arepera* (Andes)

drag queen
un travestí ; una reina

Did you see him **fagging out** at the party last night?
*¿Lo viste **volteándose** anoche en la fiesta?*

LOVEY-DOVEY NICKNAMES)))
AMORÍFICOS

My baby	*Mi amor*
My better half	*Mi media naranja*
My sweetheart	*Mi corazón*
The apple of my eye	*Alma de mi vida*
My old man	*Mi mareado* [Mex]
My sweetie	*Mi cariño*
My old lady	*Mi negra**[Arg]
Dear	*Mi querido/a***
Cutie (female)	*Mi bonbón*

* This term has, in most contexts, lost any [conscious] racial meaning it historically had.
** In Argentina, men openly call each other this —everywhere else it's strictly for lovers.

He's totally bent.
*Es un **volteado** total.*

I bet she plays for both teams.
*Ella debe **jugar en las dos direcciones.***

Manuel's wifey is a banker named Ezekiel.
*El **hembrito** de Manuel es un banquero que se llama Ezequiel.*

·····Sweet talkin'
Galanteando

To flirt
Coquetear ; Flirtear

To hit on
Ligar

To pick up
Levantar

Give me a holler.
Dame un toque. ; Dame un silbito.
Silbito means "a whistle."

Can I get your number?
¿Me darías tu número?

What's your sign?
¿Tu signo cuál es?

Can I buy you a drink?
¿Te compro algo para beber?

What are you doing tonight?
¿Tienes planes para la noche?

How was your date last night?
¿Cómo te fue la cita de anoche?

She is such a flirt.
Ella es una coqueta fatal.

Let's spend the night together.
¿Por qué no pasamos la noche juntos?

CHAPTER 3

PARTY SPANISH

CASTELLANO FIESTERO

Spanish speakers will party for any reason and without warning. These little lessons will show how to pick your path through *partilandia* without dumping on anyone's vibe, which is to say, *sin echar agua en la fiesta de nadie*.

·····Where the party at?
¿Dónde hay pachanga?

The word *fiesta* is a general term that includes the craziest bachelor party of your life, as well as your kid sister's 12th birthday party (not to be confused with her 15th, which you might actually want to go to). Know what you're being invited to before you give a yea or a nay.

I wanna…
Quiero…

go out tonight!
salir esta noche!

go all out tonight.
largar con todo esta noche.

get some ass tonight.
ligar esta noche.

do something!
hacer algo!

I think I'll just…
Me antoja más…

take it easy tonight.
pasarla tranqui esta noche.

stay home.
quedarme en casa nomás.

hit the hay.
retirarme ya.

sit this one out.
dejarla pasar a esta.

be a bum and watch TV.
hacerme el vago y quedarme con la tele.

hit the sack.
irme al sobre.

We should hit up that…
Debemos meternos en ese/esa…

Wanna crash a…?
¿Quieres colarte en un/una…?

house party
pachanga (Mex) | *jarana* (Spn)

block party
festividad de barrio

dance club
disco club (Spn) | *boliche* (S.Cone, Andes)

dive bar
antro barato (Mex)

fun little shindig among friends
party ; pari

little party in someone's apartment
fiestita depto

A TOTAL FRee-FOR-ALL)))
UN LÍO TOTAL

Here are some terms for those parties that require serious mopping-up or deep carpet cleaning, if not bail posting, afterward.

A huge blow-out	*Un reventón*
A real riot	*Un bochinche*
Utter chaos	*Un barullo*
A first-rate megaparty	*Un festejón de primera*
A rager	*Un bacanal*
No holds barred	*Deschavetado* [LatAm]

BBQ
asado (CenAm) | *barbacoa* (Carib)

ranch party
fiesta ranchera ; fiesta de quinta (more upscale)
These are massive ragers where everyone crashes in a huge ranch house—no neighbors, no cops—for days on end.

high-roller party
fiesta paquete

golden wedding anniversary celebration
festejo del aniversario de oro

masquerade
baile de máscaras
These are still common, though mostly just in bordellos these days.

·····Having fun?
¿Divertiéndote?

An important part of taking someone out is checking in and taking measurements on the fun-o-meter. Here's some vocab useful for that kind of shiz.

> You **having fun**?
> *¿Estás **disfrutando**?*

Yeah, this place doesn't suck.
Wow, genial, este lugar.
Wow, pronounced flatly enough, is clearly sarcastic even
through the worst accent.

This little place is bumpin'!
*¡Este rinconcito está **a toda madre**!* (Mex)

I feel like cutting loose.
*Me da por **vacilar**.*

Check out all the hotties!
*¡Mírale las **bomboncitas**!*

This place is super chill.
*El lugar está **rebueno**.*

Let's go…!
¡Vámonos…!

> **hit on some girls/some guys**
> *a ligarnos unas chicas / unos chavos* (LatAm) |
> *unos tiós* (Spn)

> **get a drink**
> *a echar un trago*

> **get our groove on**
> *a soltar una juerga*

get crunk
a deschavetarnos (LatAm)

home
a casa

somewhere else
a otra parte

get the fuck outta here
lejos de esta mierda

I'm **really digging** what the DJ is spinning.
*Estoy **gozando mucho** lo que está tocando el DJ.*

Check it out, your friend's really **getting down!**
*¡Éjele, que tu amigo está **vacilando**!*

Yeah, she's **grinding all over** that guy.
*Sí, ella le está **haciendo un buen perreo**.*

This place is seriously **a dive!**
*En serio que este lugar es **un tugurio**.*
Literally, "a shepherd's hut."

Yeah man, **it blows.**
*Simón, **es una mierda**.*

Let's get out of this **shithole**.
*Larguémonos de este **pedorreo**.*

Let's bounce.
Huímonos.

·····Cheers
Salud

As part of Europe, Spain has a culture of hard drinking similar to our Anglo-American one. Social interactions are often well-lubricated, complete with drinking songs and games. In Latin America, however, binge drinking is seen as more pathetic or self-destructive than social or funny, and having one too many isn't usually something to brag about the way it is in American frat culture.

Let's go for a drink.
*Vámonos para **un trago**.* | *...**un chupo**.* (S.Cone)

Wanna knock back a few?
*¿Quieres **echar unas copas**?* | *...**unos copetes**?* (Chi)

> **Cheers! A toast!**
> *¡Salud! ¡Brindis!*
>
> **To good friends!**
> *¡Brindemos por los amigotes!*
>
> **To Pancho Villa, and his rebel 'stache!**
> *¡A Pancho Villa, y su bigote bandido!*
>
> **Bottoms up!**
> *¡Arriba, abajo, al centro, y adentro!*
> Say the words to this toast as you move your glass high
> (*arriba*), low (*abajo*), toward the center (*al centro*), and then
> into your mouth in one quick drag.

Customer service can be incomparably more casual in a
Spanish restaurant than in its Latin American equivalent, and
nowhere more so than in bars, where a bartender might even
address you as "shorty" or "wise guy." It's just one more way
that the culture of alcohol is far less universal than decades of
advertising would have you believe.

> **What'll it be?**
> *¿Qué quieres?* (Spn)
>
> **What can I get you, sir?**
> *¿Qué le puedo servir al señor?* (LatAm)
>
> **Gimme...**
> *Dame...*
>
>> **a beer.**
>> *una cerveza.*
>>
>> **a brewskie.**
>> *una chela.* (LatAm) | *una birra.* (S.Cone, Andes) |
>> *una cheve.* (Mex)
>>
>> **a cheap beer.**
>> *una cerveza barata.*

a third-rate beer.
una cerveza de tercera.

a beer on tap.
una cerveza tirada.

a bottle of beer.
una botella de cerveza.

a shot.
un trago carto. | un traguito chupito. (Spn) |
un caballito. (Mex)

a glass of wine.
una copa de vino.

Let's pound these shots.
Tráguemonos estos traguitos.

Hey, bartender, a round for my friends.
*Oye, camarero, **una ronda** para mis amigos.*

Chug! Chug! Chug!
¡Traga! ¡Traga! ¡Traga!

Do you have anything on tap?
*¿Tienes algo **tirado**?*
Tirar is the verb for pulling the tap, so draft drinks are "pulled"
drinks.

Shitty beer
Cervezuela

Watery beer
Cervezagua

Let's pop some bubbly to that!
¡Adelante con las burbujas!

•••••Hard liquor
Aguardientes

With so many gloriously fermentable ingredients at their disposal, Spanish speakers have a plethora of specialty drinks that they can make like no others.

Barkeep, set me up with a splash of...
Mozo, alcánzame un chorro de...

Tequila
Made from the blue agave or *maguey* cactus, tequila has been central to Mexican drunkenness since pre-Columbian times, when drinking *pulque* (an undistilled form you can still get in some rural areas) was a sacred and often hallucinogenic way of worshipping *Mayáhuel*, the goddess of rowdiness, fertility, and peeing yourself in public.

Mezcal
Jalisco may have a trademark on *tequila*, but old-school Oaxaca's got its own variation: the *pulque*-like and earthy *mezcal* in which swims the larva of the famous *hypopta agavis* worm. Yum!

Daquirí
OK, maybe you think it's tacky because it's been your mom's favorite drink since that *Princess* cruise to Miami. But hey, in climates where fresh, ripe fruit is dirt-cheap and available year-round, it belongs in your cocktail.

¡Cuba Libre!
Somehow squeezing half a lime into a rum-n-Coke is a quantum leap forward. It also gives you a cool slogan to shout in public. But be careful, the name comes from the revolution *before* The Revolution, so you might wanna call it a *ron*

con coca y lima if you're actually in Cuba ordering this with Communist Party members around.

Telegrama

If you like mint but think mojitos and juleps are too sweet, maybe you'll like this rum and crème de menthe on ice.

Calambuco

A Cuban moonshine rum—though you might not wanna get too adventurous with drinks that could *blind* you.

Chicha

This is a general category of Andean corn-based drinks, usually but not always fermented and alcoholic. In Peru, old women sometimes start the fermentation process by chewing on the corn and spitting it out. Mmmmmm, nothing beats old lady spit!

Pisco Sour

Peru's famous distilled brandy *pisco* is mysteriously mellowed out when you add it to whipped raw egg whites, simple syrup, a dash of bitters, and the juice of a very acidic Peruvian lime.

Sangría

Many of Spain's full-bodied wines are fierce and vinegary, particularly those on the vast low end of the price spectrum. That's why adding melty ice, sweet fruit like apples, and a tart middleman like blood-orange juice isn't just a good idea, it's a goddamn national treasure.

Vodka
Vodka

Whiskey
Whisky

Gin
Ginebra

Rum
Ron

Champagne
Champán ; Champaña

Cocktail
Cóctel ; Cubata
Cubata was originally slang for *cuba libre*, but now it's slang for any mixed drink.

PARTY ALL WEEK!)))
SEMANALCOHÓLICA

Gluglunes	Glug-glug-glug
Mamartes	*Mamas*, you suck like a baby on a mammary.
Miercolitros	Liters and liters of the stuff
Juevebes	And you drink.
Beviernes	And you drink, all week, and on the weekend...
Sabadrink	Let's have a drink!
Dormingo	Sleep it off!

Girly drink
Una bebida de nenas

Virgin drink
Una bebida de monjas
Even child actresses drink in Latin America—Shirley Temples are only for nuns from the stricter orders.

Their drinks are watered down.
Las bebidas ahí vienen aguadas.

This is some cheap tequila.
¡Qué tequililla!

I'll have a beer with a whiskey chaser.
Dame una cerveza con un remate de whiskey.

I'd like a whiskey with a mineral water chaser.
Para mí, un whisky con cháser de agua mineral.
No, that's not a typo; that's how we borrow the word, confusingly enough!

·····Drunkenness
Borrachera

Try extra hard to memorize these phrases. By the time you actually need them, there's no way in hell you'll be able to pull out this book and look 'em up.

I'm...
Estoy...

American girls love to get...
A las chicas norteamericanas les encanta ponerse...

> **drunk.**
> *borracho/a.* | *cuete.* (Mex)
>
> **buzzed.**
> *achispadito/a.*
>
> **tipsy.**
> *choborra.*
> Scrambling syllables makes things cutesy and adds a wink-wink connotation, in this case conveying more affection and less judgment than *borracho*. It's not more or less drunk, it's just less pathetic.
>
> **well-done.**
> *cocido/a.* (S.Cone, Spn)
>
> **shitfaced.**
> *mamado/a.* | *doblado.* (Spn)
>
> **sloppy drunk.**
> *picado/a.* ("minced") | *taja* (Spn)
>
> **pickled.**
> *curado/a.*
>
> **wasted.**
> *fumigado/a.* (Mex) | *punto* (Spn)

Last night we all got totally trashed.
*Anoche todos **nos pusimos pedos**.* (LatAm) | *...**se agarró un pedo**.* (S.Cone)
Pedo literally means "fart," and anything done *al pedo* is done pointlessly or blindly.

Last night we went on a binge.
*Anoche **fuimos de juerga**. | ...**decuete**.* (Mex)

We were drinking everything in sight.
Nos chupamos hasta el agua del inodoro.

I can't even remember driving drunk.
*Ni siquiera me acuerdo haber **conducido cuete**.* (Mex) |
*...**manejado moña**.* (Spn)

Sounds like a serious bender.
*Suena como **un vinagre** serio.* (Spn) | *...**una curda**...*
(S.Cone)

That fool is such a/an...
Ese jil es un...total.

> **lush**
> *beodo*

> **happy drunk**
> *happy*

> **alkie**
> *borrachín*

> **boozer**
> *bebedor/a | chuzo* (Spn)

·····The morning after
La mañana siguiente

Of course, all this cirrhosis-inducing drunkenness has its
consequences.

> **I'm about to...**
> *Estoy a punto de...*

>> **throw up.**
>> *largar.*

>> **puke.**
>> *buitrear.* (CenAm, Andes, S.Cone)

>> **projectile vomit.**
>> *lanzar.*

pass out.
desmayarme.

I have a splitting hangover.
*Tengo una **cruda aguda**. | ...un **guayabo agudo**.*
("guava tree") (Andes)

He's/She's hung over.
*Él/Ella está **crudo/a**. (CenAm) | ...**enguayabado/a**.*
(Andes)

I got mean dry-mouth today.
*Hoy tengo una **secona** feroz.*

I got so drunk last night I pissed the bed.
*Me emborraché tanto anoche que **me meé en la cama**.*

Did we have sex last night?
¿Echamos algo anoche?

I don't remember shit about last night.
De anoche no me acuerdo un carajo.

I feel like ass.
Me siento como la mierda.

I gotta sleep off this buzz.
Necesito dormir la mona.

I've got the spins.
Estoy todo mareado.
As in, I just got off a boat after a shaky day on the open *mar*.

I'm so nauseous, man.
Estoy todo descompuesto, compa'.

I'm never drinking again.
Nunca más voy a tocar bebida.

·····Cancersticks
Tubitos de cáncer

Tobacco may be persecuted in the First World, but when you stray off the beaten path in the tourist-loving Third World you'll find that people couldn't give a shit about secondhand smoke. Since, you know, they have to worry about other problems like famine and guerrilla warfare and whatnot. Whether you love the stuff or want cigarettes eradicated from our planet, here are the terms you'll need to know.

You smoke?
¿Fumas?

You gotta light?
¿Tienes fuego?

You sell smokes?
¿Vendes zafiros? (Mex)

Can you spare a cig?
¿Te sobra un faso? (S.Cone)

Can I bum a cigarette?
¿Te puedo deber un fallo? (Andes)

Not a single cancerstick?
¿Ni un cáncer?

Just one drag!
¡Un toque nomás! | ...plon... (Andes)

Not even from the butt?
¿Ni siquiera del pucho?

Can I use your lighter?
¿Me prestes un encendedor?

You're a fiend. You must smoke like a chimney.
Eres un maniático. Debes fumar como una chimenea.

Yeah, I chain-smoke like a whore in the slammer.
Sí, fumo uno tras otro como puta encarcelada.

Could you stop exhaling in my direction?
¿Podrías parar de soplar por aquí?

I'm trying to quit.
Quiero dejarlo.

·····Marijuana
Marejuancho

Spanish speakers have thousands of variants for talking about Mary Jane, from *mare-juancho* ("makes-Johnny-dizzy") to *mariguano* to *marihuan* to *mora* ("berry," the cutesy variant of the Mexican *mota*).

Weed
Mota (Mex)

Bud
La marimba (Andes)

Herb
La hierba ; La hierbabuena

Hash
La grifa | *El costo* (Spn)

> **I'm feeling all hashed out.**
> *Me siento **grifo** del todo.*

Wanna smoke a joint?
*¿Quiéres fumarte **un pito**?*
Pito also means "tube" and "rod," so you can imagine the double entendres.

Let's roll a fatty.
*Dale, hagámonos un **porro gordito**.*

When are we gonna roll that spliff?
*¿Cuándo vamos a liar ese **canuto**?*

Toke that roach!
*¡Tóquete ese **puchito**!* | *...**bacha**!* (Mex)

Should we hotbox it?
*¿Debemos **hornearlo**?*

I'm so high, dude.
*Estoy tan **fumadito**, huevón.*

Man, do I love smokin' dope.
Como me gusta fumetear.

You look nicely baked.
Te ves bien arrebata'o. (Carib)

I only took one hit!
¡Solo tomé un toque!

Nah, I'm just a bit lightheaded.
Nada, es un toque de la pálida.

Whatever, you're a pothead.
Ni modo, eres un/una fumero/a.

At least I'm not a burnout.
Por lo menos no soy un/una quemado/a. (S.Cone)

If you say so, potheaderino.
Si tú lo dices, fumanchero/a.

I gotta hit up my dealer.
Necesito pegarle una llamada al vendedor. |
...vendemota. (Mex)

I got a mad case of the munchies.
Mariguantojando. | *Motantojando.* (Mex)
Mariguana + antojando (craving).

·····Doped up
Puesto

Although much of America's hard drugs come from Latin America, using the hard stuff is pretty rare in the developing world, and none too openly discussed either, given the steep penalties for possession in *any* quantity. Still, here's some handy slang for substances people use to sully the temples of their bodies.

Snort a bump.
Jalar un toquito.

Where can I score some…?
¿Dónde puedo conseguirme…?

pills
pastis | chocho (Mex)

coke
perico | farlopa (Spn)

blow
perica (LatAm) | *blanquita* (Andes) | *frula* (Arg) |
merca (S.Cone)

snow
nieve

powder
talco
As in, talcum powder.

high-octane coke
mosca (Mex)

rock
piedra basuco (Andes)

a bag of "white" (coke)
una bolsita de "blanquito"

horse (heroin)
el caballo jaco (Spn) | *chiva* (Mex)

roofies / nightynights / date-rape drugs
burundungas

ecstasy
éxtasis (Mex) | *tacha* (Mex) | *rola* (Carib)

Xanax
palitroques

G-rock
un grapa (Mex)

dime bag
un pase (Col)

Coked up
Empericado (LatAm)

You ain't nothing but a…
No eres más que un/una…

cokehead.
angurri. | *enfarlopado/a.* (Spn)

horsehead.
yonqui. (Spn)

dope fiend.
drogata.

junky.
tecato/a. (Mex) | *falopero/a.* (S.Cone) | *jincho/a.* (Spn)

They just went to the bathroom to do lines.
*Se fueron al baño a **jalar rayas**.*

He's sweating like that 'cuz he's kicking.
*Suda así por **la malilla**.* (CenAm) | *...**el mono**.* (Spn)

That shit must be good cuz that boy is trippin'.
*Debe ser bueno eso porque ese chico está **volando**.* |
*...**del otro lado**.* (Carib, Spn)

You are tweaking, bro!
*¡Estás **volando**, mano!*

Don't drink that beer! I think that scumbag tried to roofy you.
*¡No tomes esa cerveza! Me parece que ese reo intentó **emburundangarte**.*

·····Houses of ill repute
Casas libertinas

Prostitution, though technically illegal, is alive and well in Latin America, God bless its liberal soul. Even if you're not planning on hitting up any brothels in your travels, it never hurts to know what they're called, particularly since these terms are often jokingly used to refer to a really bangin' party that has an awesome girl-to-guy ratio.

Who wants to go to a cabaret? (burlesque or dancing establishment)
*¿Quién quiere ir a un **cabaré**?*

Sure, as long as it's not a **crab-eret.** (no stage or dance floor, just a straight-up brothel)
*Bueno, con que no sea un **cabarute**.*

Could we compromise on a **gentlemen's club**?
*¿Y si transijamos en una **casa de idolatría**?*

Fine, let's roll to the **titty bar.**
*Vale, larguémonos al **antro de vicioso**.*

Me too, I'm down for the **strip club**, but let's skip the **brothel**.
*Yo también, estoy listo para el **estripclub**, pero no un **burdel**.*

Seriously, I got crabs at the last **whorehouse**.
*En serio, me tocaron ladillas en la última **ramería**.*

Man, that's because that place was a **crackwhore-house.**
*Chavón, es porque ese lugar era una **chinchería**. | …**piringundín**.* (S.Cone)

How much for an hour?
¿Cuánto la hora?

Prostitute
Pelandusca

Hooker
Puta

Street walker
Yira (S.Cone)

Pimp
Proxenata

·····Don't be a snitch!
¡No seas soplón!

Unless your idea of tourism involves seeing the inside of a Third World prison (not recommended), you may wanna study up on these important bywords for police presence.

THE GHETTOS)))
BARRIOS PERDIDOS

When you're searching for a good nightclub, you might want to avoid straying into Latin American shantytowns, which tend to be druglord-controlled autonomous zones way off the utility and police grids.

Grab your bulletproof vest and let's head to the ghetto...
Agarra tu chaleco antibalas y vámonos al/a la...

villa miseria (Arg)
población callampa (Chi)
barrio marginal (Ecu)
asentamiento (Gua)
chacarita (Par)
arrabal (PuR)
cantegril (Uru)

barrio (DoR, Ven)
tugurio (Col, CoR)
barrio de chabolas (Spn)
*ciudad perdida, nopal,
   colonia popular* (Mex)
*pueblo joven, asentamiento
   humano* (Per)

Here come the...!
¡Viene/Vienen...!

po-po
la pole

cops
la cana | *la tomba* (Andes)

fuzz
los pacos (LatAm) | *la jura* (Mex)

pigs
los cuicos (Mex) | *los puercos* (Carib) | *los cobanis* (S.Cone) | *los bolillos* (Col)

Fuck the police!
¡A la mierda con la pole!

It wasn't me, I swear!
¡Yo no fui, lo juro!

Hide your stash!
*¡Esconde el **clavo**!* (Mex) | *...la **clatera**!* (Andes)

Oh shit, they're using the billy clubs!
¡Mierda, están usando las porras! | …los bolillos! (Andes, S.Cone)

They're gonna put us all in lockup!
¡Nos van a meter todos en cana!

Damn, they nabbed Pookie and took him away in cuffs.
Agarraron a Pookie y se lo llevaron engrillado.

He's gonna end up in the joint.
Va a terminar en el bote.

Well, he best remember that snitches get stitches.
Le convendría acordarse que los batidores salen bien batidos. (S.Cone)

CHAPTER 4

BODY SPANISH
CASTELLANO CORPORAL

•••••Hey, Fatso!
¡Oye, Gordo!

Spanish speakers are pretty blunt when describing each other's physical characteristics. Someone with a big beard is called Beardy, someone shaped like a pear is called…Pear. A well-hung man is called…. You get the point.

Hey…!
¡Oye…!

bignose
narigón/ona

flatnose
ñata
This often carries a potentially racist connotation of having native blood.

mangaeyes
focojos
Literally, "spotlight."

one-eye
tuerto/a
To say "look the other way" in Spanish, you'd say *se hace tuerto*, which is pretty funny if you think about it.

one-arm
manco/a
Saying *no es manco* ("he's not one-armed") about someone means they're handy.

baldy (shaved)
pelado/a

baldy (male-pattern)
calvito
From *calvo*, "skull."

baldy (lookin' like a cancer patient)
pelón de hospicio
As in, shaved for lice at the shelter!

bighead
coco grande

egghead
cocudo
Literally, "coconut to spare."

bushybeard
barbudo

Mick Jagger mouth
jetón/ona

fatlips
bembón/ona (LatAm)
Bembón refers to a racially West African "look" and/or puffy, swollen lips—be careful with either connotation.

bigass
nalgón/ona

bigtits
pechona | *chichuda* (Mex)

birthin' hips
caderota

fatbelly
panzón/ona

old saggy (fem.)
Adelcaida

shorty
bajito

dwarf / little guy
petiso

midget
enano/a

short stack
chato/a
Careful when using this one—it implies stockiness, not just compactness!

pip-squeak
tapón
Literally, "sink-stopper" or "earplug."

big, bulky dude
grandote

giant
gigante

beanpole
langaruto

toothpick (as in, unhealthy)
enclenque | *tílico/a* (Mex) | *fifiriche* (CenAm)

·····The whole package
El paquete entero

Here are the standards to describe the people who float your boat. When traveling, be sure to pay attention to local terms for hot men and women, because every region of every Spanish-speaking country has its own unique words. A lot are based on local food vocabulary—*una torta, una manteca, un churro, un chile, una chilera…*

He / She…
Él / Ella…

   is fine.
   es fina.

is adorable.
es preciosa.

is gorgeous.
es espléndida.

will make you drool.
es para babearse.

will leave you speechless.
te deja atónito.

is very sexy.
es bien sexy.

is hot shit.
es lo más.

is in shape.
está cuajado/a. (Col)

That girl **is hot.**
*Esa chica **está buena**.* | *...**es maciza**.* (Spn)

She's a **stone fox.**
*Es una **buenota**.*

Your mom's a **ten**, buddy.
*Tu vieja es **un cuero**, macho.*

Your sister's a **cutey.**
*Tu hermana es un **bizcocho**.* (Mex)

Is it weird to think that Steve Urkel is **a total hunk?**
*¿Es raro pensar que Steve Urkel es **un buenón total**?*

What a **hotty!**
*¡Que **cuerazo**!*

Ohmigod, there are, like, so many **hot guys** here.
*¡Epa, mira los tantos **papis** que hay por aquí!* |
*...**papuchos**...* (Mex)

I love men with **big guns.**
*Como quiero a los hombres con **brazos macizos**.*

Your little brother is ripped!
*¡Tu hermanito está **fornido**! | ...**mamado**!* (Mex)
In the Southern Cone, *mamado* means drunk or permanently brain-damaged by drinking.

Damn, he is so cut!
*¡Ufa, que está **bien dado**! | ...**manga**!* (Col) |
...***calote**!* (Mex)

Lookin' slim!
*¡Te ves **delgado/a**!*

Are you a swimmer? You've got a good, toned build.
*¿Nadas? Tienes un **buen lomo**.*

My girl's / guy's got...
Mi novi' tiene...

> **a good figure.**
> *una buena figura. | un buen lomo.* (S.Cone)
>
> **a bangin' body.**
> *un cuerpazo.*
>
> **a hot bod.**
> *un cuerpo estelar.*
>
> **a narrow waist.**
> *una cintura ancha.*
>
> **an hourglass figure.**
> *un cuerpo de guitarra.*
> Literally, "a body of a guitar."
>
> **nice legs.**
> *buenas gambas.*
> The old East Coast slang, "gams," comes from the same Italian word.
>
> **gorgeous eyes.**
> *ojos deslumbrantes.*
>
> **big doe eyes.**
> *ojotes de coneja.*

•••••Fugly
Defeorme

Because sometimes you just gotta tell it like it is.

The thing is, he's just fucking ugly.
*Lo que tiene, es que es **feo como la mierda***.

Damn! She's heinous!
*¡Carajo! ¡Es **atroz**!*

Is it just me, or is Mary Kate kind of formless?
*¿Es cosa mía, o es Mary Kate un poco **amorfa**?*

> **At least she's not frumpy.**
> *Por lo menos no es **babosa**.*
> Literally, a "slug."

Dude, your dad is so hairy!
*Hombre, ¡que **peludo** es tu viejo!*

He's a little chubby in the cheeks for my tastes.
*Para mí, él es un poco **fofito en las mejillas**.*

What've you been eating, tubby?
*¿Qué estás comiendo, **fofo/a**?*

What a lardass!
*¡Qué **gordinflón/ona**!*

> **Hey, don't start with me, Pillsbury.**
> *Epa, no te metas conmigo, **Michelin**.*

I have a major double chin in this pic.
*Tengo **una papada real** en esta foto.*

Ugh, you want me to talk to that hunchback?
*Ufa, ¿quieres que hable yo con ese/a **jorobado/a**?*

Were you born bowlegged?
*¿Naciste **rengo/a**?*

> **You're walking like a cowboy, chief.**
> *Estás **rengueando**, jefe/a.*

THE BRAIN BOWL)))
EL TAPASESOS

For some strange reason, phrases for some body parts are totally standard across all dialects of Spanish, while others vary wildly from place to place. Given how often Spanish speakers hit each other upside the head, maybe it makes sense to have so many nicknames for it.

Term	Literal Meaning	Used In...
balero	magazine (for bullets, *balas*)	S.Cone
bocha	from Italian *boccia*, bowl	S.Cone
capocha	from Italian *capoccia*, head	Arg
chirimoya	a small, head-shaped fruit	Mex
cholla, choya	intelligence, judgment	Universal
coco	coconut	Universal
jupa	--	CenAm
marote, marulo	--	S.Cone
mate	gourd for drinking yerba	Par, Uru
mitra	miter	Per
moropo	--	Carib
ñola	--	CenAm
olla	cooking pot	Spn
sesera	brain (*sesos*) cavity	Universal
tarro	pot (like for mustard)	Spn
tutuma	from Quechua	Andes
xola	from Mayan	CenAm

Sorry, but she's not skinny, she's skeletal.
*Disculpe, pero ella no está flaca, está **esquelética**.*

You look like an emaciated P.O.W.
*Pareces un/a prisionero/a **enclenque**. | ...**tílico/a**.* (Mex)

I'm not into the whole boniness thing.
*No me da por todo ese asunto de **la flaquencia**.*
Flaquencia can also be used as a polite way to insinuate an eating disorder.

She's got a great body, but a face like a cockatoo.
*Tiene buena carrocería, pero con **cara de cacatúa**.*

Did you see that mug?
*¿Viste a esa **careta**? | …**caripela**.* (S.Cone)

Check out four-eyes.
*Mírale **cuatr'o ojos**. | …**piticiego**.* (Chi)

It's sad he has such a Pinocchio nose.
*Es una lástima **la cayuya** que tiene.* (Chi) | *…**tocha**…*
(Spn) | *…**napia**…* (S.Cone)

That comb-over just isn't working.
*¡Qué mal queda ese **emparrado**!*
Literally, "a lattice for growing beans or vines."

You've got big ol' horse teeth.
*¡Qué **jachas**!* (CenAm) | *¡Qué **piños**!* (Spn)

Hey, gaptooth!
*¡Oye, **chimuelo**!* (Mex, CenAm)

Is he picking on that toothless old lady?
*¿Él se burla de esa vieja **xolca**?* (CenAm) | *…vieja **mellá**?*
(Carib)

·····Stylin'
Engalaneado

What good is your slammin' body if you're dressed in a sack and haven't changed your drawers in six days? Here are some handy phrases for describing the styled—or inadequately styled, as the case may be.

> **He/She looks…**
> *Él/Ella se ve…*
>
>> **fashionable.**
>> *galano/a.*
>>
>> **put-together.**
>> *bien compuesto/a.*

well-tailored.
a la tela.

sharp.
prolijo/a.

preened.
prolijito/a.

O.C.D. (as in, your shoelaces match your belt, bag, underwear, and eye shadow)
T.O.C. (trastorno obsesivo-compulsivo)

unkempt.
descuidado/a.

sloppy.
desaliñado/a.

threadbare.
deshilachado/a.

like a real mess.
bien abandonado/a.

·····Tits and ass
Tetas y culo

The Eskimos, it's said, developed over 100 words for snow because they've been surrounded by the terrible, freezing stuff every moment of their miserable lives. Ergo, Spanish speakers must be up to their ears in sweet, delicious ass because they have more ways to describe *booty* than the ancient Greeks had gods.

You have a great bust.
*Tienes un **delantero** tremendo.*

Play with my…
Juega con mis…

You have beautiful…
Tienes unos/unas…hermosas.

Could I motorboat your…?
*¿Puedo **hacer trompetillas con** tus…?* (Mex)

breasts
senos

boobies
bubis

knockers
globos

titties
chichis (Mex)

tits
tetas (Andes) | *lolas* (S.Cone)

hooters
gemelas (Col)

She's got some perky little breasts, doesn't she?
*¿Tiene pechugitas **paraditas**, no?*

You could ski jump off those little barbs.
*Podrías hacer salto con esquis en esas **respingonas**.*

She's bursting with personal endowments.
Ella tiene una pechonalidad tremenda.

Does she have fake boobies?
¿Tiene las teclas falsas?

She is so flat-chested she looks like she hasn't even hit puberty yet.
Ella tiene el pecho tan liso que parece ni entrada en pubertad.

Those are some saggy boobs.
Están bien caidas esas tetas.

Those are just ugly boobs.
Esas son pechufeas.

She has enormous nipples.
Ella tiene pezones enormes.

His nipples are kind of wierd.
Él tiene las tetillas algo raras.

I'm in love with your…
Estoy enamorado de tu/tus…

> **derriere.**
> *trasero.*
>
> **butt.**
> *fondillo.*
>
> **bottom.**
> *poto.* (Andes)
>
> **butt cheeks.**
> *nalgas.*
>
> **heinie.**
> *pompis.* (Mex)
>
> **ass.**
> *culo.* | *traste.* (S.Cone)
>
> **fat ass.**
> *culón.*
>
> **ass crack.**
> *raya del culo.*
>
> **ass cheeks.**
> *ancas.*

buns of steel.
ancotas de plomo.

firm glutes.
tambo. (CenAm)
Tight like the head of a drum (*tambo*).

Look how she shakes that money maker!
*¡Mira como mueve el **cubilete**!*

Damn! Check out that big-booty girl with all that junk in the trunk!
*¡Pucha! ¡Mírale todo el cargo que lleva esa **nalgona**!*

Your boyfriend is totally assless.
*Tu novio es **totalmente desnalgado**.* (Mex)

I love Latinas and their big, thunderous ass cheeks.
*Como me gustan las latinas con esas **ancotas temibles** que llevan.*

I prefer British girls with those right-solid rumps.
*A mí me da más por las inglesas, con esas **ancas bien sólidas**.*

Why do Japanese chicks all have those superflat butts?
*¿Por qué tienen todas las japonesas esos **fundillos de aspirina**?*
Ever looked at an aspirin pill?

·····Spare tires
Llantas

People come in all shapes and sizes. Some are blessed with nice, tight abs. Others have stomachs that spill over their jeans like overyeasted dough. Although we can't harvest all the fatties to make candles and petroleum jelly out of their fat deposits, at least we can make up funny names for their humongous beer guts.

You sure have a soft belly.
*Tienes la **panza** muy suavecita.*

Man, your dad's really got a beer gut.
*¡Qué **guata** tiene tu viejo, hombre!* (S.Cone, Andes) |
*…**botijón**…* (CenAm)

Is that woman actually with child, or does she just have a pregger-gut?
*¿Esa mujer está con hijo de verdad, o tiene el **bombo** nomás?*

You gotta start working off that spare tire.
*Deberías liberarte de esa **llanta**.* (LatAm)

What about your muffin-top?
*¿Y tu **bollito**?*
Bollo (bun) also has a lot of local usages: "turd" in Colombia, "dyke" in Spain, "vulva" in Cuba…

Nice six-pack! Do you work out?
*¡Linda **tabla de chocolate**! ¿Haces ejercicios?*

> **Nah, these washboard abs just come natural.**
> *Psh, este **tabla de lavar** vino así.*

·····Piss and shit
Pis y mierda

Like most bodily functions in the Spanish-speaking world, the acts of peeing and pooping aren't considered scandalous enough to generate much eloquence or circumlocution. Everyone poops, right? So why get all worked up about it?

> **I gotta…**
> *Necesito…*

hit the john.
irme al trono.

drain the lizard.
achicar la verga.

tinkle.
hacer pipí. | *hacer chichi.* (Col) | *puchar.* (S.Cone)

take a piss.
mear.

mark some territory.
poner la firma.

take a shit.
cagar.

drop a turd.
depositar un zurullo. | *...sorete.* (S.Cone)

drop off a dung delivery.
dejar una entrega de estiércol.

I...
Yo...

am constipated.
estoy estreñido.

have diarrhea.
tengo una cursera. ; tengo churras.

have the shits.
tengo la cagadera.

have the runs.
tengo un chorrillo. (Mex) | *estoy de carreritas.* (Carib)

left skid marks on my drawers.
dejé un sello en los calzones.

I got drunk and pissed myself.
Me emborraché hasta mearme todo.

Wake up, before you wet the bed.
Despiértate antes que te mees en la cama.

**I'd wait a while before you go in there. I just dropped
a deuce.**
*Yo por tí esperaría un cacho. Acabo de hacer
del dos.* (Mex)

It smells awful. **Did you shit yourself?**
¡Qué aliento! ¿Te cagaste?

·····Bodily fluids
Fluidos corporales

Spanish speakers don't actually have much slang for bodily
fluids. They're kind of nonchalant about them, unlike the
British, who think that the ridiculous word "bloody" is the
worst thing you could ever say to a person. The lesson, as
usual: Brits are weird.

Earwax
Cerilla

Unplug your ears, jackass!
¡Sácate la vela de las orejas, jil!

Snot
Moco

I have a terrible **runny nose.**
*Tengo una **moquera** terrible.*

He **got the snot knocked out of him** in that
accident.
Se hizo moco en ese accidente.

That **little snot-nose** just ran off with my bike
seat!
*¡Ese **mocoso** acaba de llevarse el asiento de mi bici!*

Wipe off your **eyeboogers,** you mouthbreather!
*¡Quítate las **legañas**, baboso!*

Your **eyecrust** revolts me.
*Tu **graña** me da asco.*

Your **pimples** are getting out of control.
*Tus **espinillas** se están desbordando.*

You need to **pop those zits** before your face
explodes.
*Tienes que **apretarte esos granos** antes de que te
explote la cara. | ...**barros**... (Carib)*

Everyone **gets blackheads** now and then.
*A todos **nos salen granitos** de vez en cuando.*

Is that **drool**?
*¿Son **babas**?*

Don't **drool all over yourself,** that's my sister!
*¡No **te babees todo**, esa es mi hermana!*

Spit it out, it's nasty!
*¡**Escúpelo**, está asqueroso!*

To menstruate
Reglar

I have **menstrual cramps.**
*Tengo **los cólicos**.*

Her **monthly visitor** came.
*Le vino **la regla**.*

Aunt Flo is visiting.
***Don Goyo** está de visitas.* (Carib)

Don't start with her, she's **on the rag** somethin' fierce.
*No metes pata, está **monstruando** bien serio.*

Do you have an extra **tampon**?
*¿Te sobra un **tampón**?*

All they have are **pads** in this fucking country!
*¡En este puto país no hay mas que **toallas sanitarias**!*

·····Other bodily functions
Otras funciones corporales

Damn you just **ripped** one!
*¡Carajo, acabas de **largar** uno!*

Sorry, I just let out a **silent but deadly.**
*Disculpe, acabo de **zurrar**.* (S.Cone)
Careful, though: Outside of the Southern Cone, this refers to involuntary incontinence.

That's OK, I'll return fire with a loud tooter.
*Está bien, te devuelvo fuego con un **cuete**.* (LatAm)

I'm terribly gassy.
Estoy con un gas tremendo.

Uhhhh! Who farted?
*¿Uuuuu, quién se **cuescó**?* (Spn)

I bet I can burp louder than you.
*Te apuesto que **eructo** más fuerte que tú.*

Dude, you've got some rank B.O.
*Hombre, tienes un **grajo** que espanta.* (CenAm, Carib) |
*...una **baranda**...* (S.Cone) | *...un **cante**...* (Spn)

How's my breath?
*¿Cómo está mi **aliento**?*

Saying my dad snores is an understatement; he's a sawmill!
*Decir que mi viejo **ronca** sería quedarse corto; ¡es un aserradero!*

I used to grind my teeth in my sleep.
*Antes **rechinaba los dientes** cuando dormía.*

I got cramps in my leg last night.
*Me agarraron **calambres** en las piernas anoche.*

Stand me up, I'm all dizzy from smoking so much pot.
*Párame, que estoy todo **mareado** de tanto fumetear.*

She's preggers.
*Está **encinta**. ; ...**preñada**.*

He put some bread in her oven.
Él le llenó la cocina de humo.
Literally, "He filled her kitchen with smoke."

Did you take a home pregnancy test?
*Hiciste la **prueba de embarazo casera**?*

·····Ailments
Achaques

If you're a true traveler to Latin America, you'll encounter plenty of spicy food, hard liquor, outdoor plumbing, and disease-carrying mosquitoes. Add 'em all up and chances are you're gonna get sick. But it all makes for a better story when you get home, so stop your sniveling and eat the worm already!

I feel awful.
Me siento pésimo.

I feel like balls.
*Me siente como el **orto**. ; …el **culo**.*

He is so ill.
Él está muy mal.

I'm so nauseous.
Tengo nauseas tan fuertes.

Move, I'm gonna…!
¡Múevete, que voy a…!

> **throw up**
> *echar buitre* (LatAm)
>
> **upchuck**
> *buitrear* (LatAm)
>
> **puke**
> *trallar*
>
> **hurl**
> *guasquear* (Andes) | *huacarear* (Mex)

How did I end up covered in vomit?
*¿Cómo terminé **cubierto en vómito**?*

He'll be praying to the porcelain goddess all night.
*Va a pasarse la noche **devolviendo atenciones**.*
Literally, "writing thank-you cards."

I have a **migraine,** get me a **painkiller!**
¡Tengo jaqueca, alcánzame un calmante!

I think I got **scabies** from sleeping in that creep's bed!
¡Me parece que me tocó la sarna durmiendo en la cama de ese reo!

I have **stomach cramps** from eating all that meat.
Tengo retortijones por comer tanta carne.

He's got **a bit of a gimpy leg,** right?
Tiene la pierna medio coja, ¿verdad?

> Is he still **walking with a limp?**
> *¿Sigue cojeando?*

Do you wanna see my **bruises?**
¿Quieres ver mis moretones?

Those are **bite marks!**
¡Esos son mordiscos!

I need some...
Necesito...

> **strong drugs.**
> *drogas fuertes.*
>
> **Ibuprofen.**
> *Ibuprofeno.*
>
> **Tylenol.**
> *Tylenol.*
>
> **laxatives.**
> *laxantes.*
>
> **antidepressants.**
> *antidepresivos.*
>
> **barbiturates.**
> *barbitúricos.*

CHAPTER 5

HORNY SPANISH
ESPAÑOL ARRECHO

Despite the Catholic heritage, sex is a big part of Spanish culture. Newsstands sell hardcore porno next to kids' comics, websites rank proudly the best sexual catcalls, and newscasters tend to be big-titted, raven-haired vamps that make Katie Couric look like a sexless, albino sloth. Because Spanish speakers are so down with sex, they don't demonize it the way Americans can. They have "natural," not illegitimate, children; tell "green" jokes instead of dirty ones; become "green" old men instead of dirty old ones; and have extramarital "adventures" instead of affairs. Not bad, considering that in most Spanish-speaking countries, divorce wasn't even legal 20 years ago.

·····Fucking 101
Coger 101

There is no universal Spanish term for fucking. Spaniards use *joder* and Mexicans use *chingar,* both of which mean "to fuck" in those countries but "to irritate" everywhere else. The rest of Latin America uses *coger*. But Spaniards never got the memo and still use *coger* in its dictionary sense of "to catch, get, or hold." This causes mass hysteria among Latin Americans whenever they hear a Spaniard talking about needing to fuck a bus. To add to the confusion, *trincar* has the opposite problem and means "to seize or grab" everywhere except for Spain where, inevitably, it means "to fuck." You might wanna draw yourself a little chart at the airport.

I wanna…
Quiero…

Do you want to…?
¿Quieres…?

Let's go and…
Vámonos a…

I'd love to…
Me gustaría…

> **have sex**
> *tener sexo*
>
> **fuck**
> *coger | chingar* (Mex) | *follar* (Spn)
>
> **screw**
> *culear | fifar* (S.Cone)
>
> **boink**
> *tirar | curtir* (S.Cone)
> *Tirar* literally means "to throw."
>
> **knob**
> *empomar*
>
> **bone**
> *joder*
> *Joder,* like the British "bugger," can mean anything from mild, nagging irritation to sodomy. Most of the time it hovers ambiguously in between.
>
> **plug her**
> *enchufarla* (Mex)
>
> **hit that**
> *comérsela | darle masa* (Andes)

nail that ass
clavar ese culo

have a fuck
echar un palo

have a double-fuck
echar un doble-palo

have a fuckathon
echar un buen caldo
Ever made broth (*caldo*) from scratch? It takes all day.

have a quickie
echar un rapidín ; un cuiqui

get your rocks off
echar un polvo (literally, "toss some powder") | *...un talco* (S.Cone)

leave it raw
fregarla (literally, "to scrub it") ; *cepillarla* (literally, "to scrub it with a cleaning brush")

hook up
ligar

pick someone up
levantarle a alguien

get involved with someone (sexually)
meterse con alguien

·····Gettin' horny
Arrechándose

A word should capture the essence of the thing it stands for. "Butterfly," for instance, sounds soft, fluttery, and beautiful. "Dump" sounds like a stinky, formless mound of crap. So you'd think that the word for orgasming would be something like "amazingawesomebestfeelingeverIloveitsomuchIwantto marryit." This isn't the case in English, though, where formal sex talk consists of excruciating words like "ejaculate" and "climax" that turn sex into some kind of science fair project. Spanish, on the other hand, uses lyrical, poetic phrases like "boil over," "outdo yourself," and "go into a frenzy" that capture the true spirit of nut-busting.

YOU SAY "FRENCH KISS," I SAY "RUSSIAN ANAL MASSAGE")))

For some reason, Spanish speakers have decided that certain nationalities are better than others at performing specific sex acts. How do they know, for instance, that the Lebanese give the world's best armpit jobs or that no one can massage an asshole like a Russian? Only the most seasoned sex tourist would know, and I'm guessing he's a native speaker.

HACERE	GIVE A/HAVE A€
una francesa	blow job
un tailandés	full-body boob massage
un croata	full-body lickdown
un serbio	full-body chompdown
un árabe	face-sitting (female on male)
un ruso	anal massage
un griego	anal sex
un romano	orgy
un japonés	floor sex (with pillows for props)
un turco	sex with recipient cuffed behind back
un libanés	armpit job
una cubana	titfuck
una pinza birmana	foot job (literally, a "Burmese grip")

Damn, girl, you're getting me all excited.
*Ufa, chica, me estás dando **un buen morbo**.* (Spn)

You make me so horny.
*Me pones tan **arrecho/a**.* (LatAm) | ...***bellaco/a***. (Carib)

I got a boner that won't quit.
*Tengo **un duro que dura**.*

I'm hard for you.
Estoy al palo para ti.

BURY THE BONE)))
HUNDIR EL HUESO

Fritar la berenjena	**Deep-fry the eggplant**
Engrasar la nutria	**Grease the marmot**
Enhebrar el hilo	**Thread the needle (i.e., anally)**
Enterrar la batata	**Bury the yam**
Medir el aceite	**Dunk the dipstick**
Revolver el estofado	**Stir the coals**
Serruchar el piso	**Saw the floor**
Peinar para adentro	**Comb it from the inside**
Ñaca-ñaca	**Hubba-hubba**
Frike-frike	**Freaky-freaky**
Dunga-dunga	**Humpy-humpy**

I want it **inside me**.
*Lo quiero **adentro**.*

Why don't we do it right here?
*¿**Por qué no lo echámos** aquí nomás?*

Tell me how you want it.
Dime como lo quieres.

Oh, you **feel so good**.
*Ooo, **estás bueno**.*

You're **so big and hard**.
*Estás **tan duro y grandón**.*

Wow, you're **really wet** today.
*¡Wow, qué estás **bien húmeda** hoy!*

You're **makin' soup in my panties**!
*¡Me estás **calentando la estufa**!*
Literally, "stoking the stove."

Come on, **faster! Harder!**
*¡Dale, **más rápido**! ¡**Más fuerte**!*

Are you close to cumming?
*¿Estás por **correrte**? ; ...**venirte**?*
Literally, "to run, flow, or brim over."

Ohmigod, I'm gonna cum!
*¡Carajo, me estoy por **llegar**!*

Cum on my face.
***Lechéame** la cara.*

Do it, then.
Hazlo, pues.

Oh yeah, take it all, you freak!
*¡Ja, **tómalo todo,** loca!*

·····Other sex acts
Otros actos sexuales

Variety is the spice of life. All good things in moderation. Man cannot live on genital sex alone. Sometimes he needs a blow job or a good circlejerk to balance his yin and yang.

Will you suck me off?
¿Me lo chuparías?

Wanna blow me?
*¿Quisieras **mamármelo**?*

I like it when you swallow my cum.
*Me gusta cuando me **tragas** la leche.*

I want you to ride me like a pony.
*Quiero que **me cabalgues** como una yegua.*

C'mon, just give me one dick-poke.
*Dale, déme un **puntazo** nomás.*

If you don't have a condom, just skeet-shoot all over me.
*Si no hay condones, **dispárame en blanco** nomás.*

Pull out at the last minute and **splash it on** my tits.
*Al fin, **ponla en marcha atrás** y **salpícame** las tetas.*

I'd like to try…
Quisiera probar…

How 'bout…?
¿Qué tal…?

Have you ever done…?
¿Has echo alguna vez…?

> **dry-humping**
> *la frottage* (from the French)
>
> **a blow job**
> *una mamada | un pete* (S.Cone)
>
> **a full-service blow job**
> *recitar el rosario*
>
> **a hand job**
> *la paja* (LatAm)
> Literally, "tumbleweed."
>
> **a circlejerk**
> *una carrera de pajas* (LatAm)
> Literally, "jackoff race."
>
> **a circlesuck**
> *una margarita*
>
> **a threesome**
> *un trío sexual*
>
> **an orgy**
> *una orgía*
>
> **a sex party**
> *el partus ; una "fiesta"*
>
> **69**
> *sesenta y nueve*
>
> **titty-fucking**
> *la paja rusa*
>
> **anal sex**
> *sexo anal*

WHAT'S YOUR FAVORITE POSITION?)))
¿CUÁL ES TU POSICIÓN FAVORITA?

Missionary	*Misionero*
Doggy-style	*La adoración*
Cowgirl	*Cabalgando*
Wheelbarrow	*La gran carretilla*
Standing T	*El cartero* ("the postman"!)
Spoon	*En caja*
Reverse cowgirl	*Cabalgando hacia atrás*
Both knees up	*La defensa amorosa*
Both legs up	*El candelabro*
Ankles on giver's shoulders	*Los abdominales* (an abs workout!)
Knees held spread	*El barco de vela* ("the galley")
Spoonee turned halfway back	*La santanderina*

backdoor action
la trastienda
Literally, "backdoor dealings."

cunnilingus
el buceo
Literally, "diving."

a snowball
un beso blanco

a rim job
un beso negro

the ol' finger in the butt
la espada de Carlomagno
Isn't "Sword of Charlemagne" more fun to say than "finger in the butt"?

a golden shower
una lluvia dorada

I'm sick of...let's fuck already.
Estoy harto de...quiero coger ya.

making out
enrollarnos (Spn) | bregarnos (Carib)

foreplay
cachondear | fajar (Mex)

cuddling
franelear (S.Cone)

third base
darnos el lote

just pawing each other
tanto magrear

fingering you
dedearte ; darte dedo

•••••Nuts and bolts
Tornillos y tuercas

Unless you're gonna be a doctor, you should probably expand your selection of sex nouns beyond the medical ones you learned in school. I wish there were space to convey the astounding richness of regional and poetic variations, but alas, a guide is not the same as an encyclopedia, which is what we'd end up with if I tried to include all the thousands of Spanish names for "junk."

Grab my...
Agárrame...

Play with my...
Manotéame...

Suck my...
Chúpame...

Touch my...
Tócame...

DiCK-TALK)))
JERGA VERGA

Tree trunk	*El tronco*
Soup can	*El marlo* (literally, "corncob")
One-eyed giant	*El chino tuerto* ("slanted eye" = urethra)
Baldy	*El pelado*
The hose	*La manguera*
The meat stick	*La butifarra, morcilla*
The stick shift	*La palanca*
Piece	*El pedazo*
Knob	*El pomo*
Limp dick	*Un pene de soga*
Little dick	*El cacahuete ; el maní* (literally, "peanut")

You have huge/a huge…
Tienes muy grande/tienes un/a grande…

privates.
los agentes.

package.
el paquete. ; el bulto. ("bundle")

nuts.
las bolas. | *los belines.* (S.Cone)

balls.
los huevos. (Mex) | *los cojones.* (Spn)

ball sac.
las talegas. (CenAm)

'nads.
las pelotas. (S.Cone)

boner.
la puntada.

dick.
el pito.

cock.
la verga. | *el bicho* (PuR)

rod.
el pijo. | *la pija.* (S.Cone) | *la polla.* (Spn)

shaft.
la pinga. | *la poronga.* (S.Cone)

prick.
el pincho.

weiner.
el nabo.

weenie.
la pirula.

Uncut
Con pellejo | *Con forro* (Carib) | *Encapuchado* (S.Cone)

Jizz
Leche | *Lefa* (Spn)

·····'Gina talk
Chochisme

Lick my…
Lámeme…

Hit my…
Méchame…

Eat my…
Cómete…

Shave my…
Aféitame…

Manhandle my…
Manotéame…

pussy.
la chocha. | *la crica.* (Carib)
The only place *chocha* doesn't mean "pussy" is in Argentina,
where it's used as an adjective to mean "stoked"!

pooch.
potorro. (Spn)

twat.
la cuca. (CenAm)

pussy lips.
el bollo. (Carib)

carpet.
la alfombrita. ; el felpudo. ("the felted bit")

bush.
el arbusto. ; la selvita. ("the little jungle")

box.
la pandorca. (Carib)

peach.
la castaña. ("chestnut")

clam.
la almeja.

cooch.
la chucha. (Andes)

poontang.
la concha. ("conch shell") (S.Cone) | *la panocha.* (Carib)

cunt.
el funciete. (Mex) | *el coño.* (Spn)
Spaniards also use *coño* as an expletive like "fuck!" or "shit!"

shaved pussy.
la chocha afeitadita. | *la chocha rasurada.* (Mex) |
la concha rapada. (S.Cone)

clit.
la campana. ("bell") ; *el botón.* ("the button")

G-spot.
el punto G.

cameltoe.
el hachazo.

perineum.
el periné.

·····Accessories
Accesorios

Sex today seems to involve all sorts of preparation and specialized equipment. Gone are the good ol' days when you just dragged your smelly ass down to the next hut, fucked like cavemen, and had a baby nine months later that probably died of hypothermia. Now you gotta have perfume, satin sheets, birth control, a Barry White album, a mirror on the ceiling, at least 10 minutes of foreplay, and a vibrator for reinforcement.

Are you on the pill?
¿Estás tomando la píldora?

Man, I miss my ex, who had an IUD.
*Como echo a menos a la ex que tenía "DIU." |
...la "T." | ...el ancla.* (literally, "the anchor")

Do you have…?
¿Tienes…?

a condom
un preservativo

a rubber
un impermeable | *un forro* (S.Cone)

any piercings
perforaciones

an STD
una venérea
You can also use this to call someone "a walking STD."

handcuffs
las esposas | *las chachas* (CenAm)

Shit! The **condom** broke!
*¡Mierda, se quebró el **forro**!*

Reach me a…
Alcánzame un/una…

Wanna try a…?
¿Quisieras probar con un/una…?

I love using a…
Me encanta usar un/una…

dildo
consolador
Consolador literally means "consolation," like for not having dick on hand when you want it.

vibrator
vibrador

tickling cockring
párpado de carba
This glorious phrase literally denotes the eyelashes of a goat. Isn't Spanish awesome?

blindfold
venda

gag
mordaza

paddle
paleta

·····Sexual sociology
La sociología sexual

It's a well-known fact that when a guy sleeps around he's a ladies' man, but if a girl gets around she ain't nothing but a slut. This double standard exists all over the world and goes to show you that, deserved or not, your sex life often comes to define you. Maybe that explains why so many homophobes are secretly gay themselves, and why the most judgmental people are usually compulsive masturbators.

That horndog would fuck anything on legs.
*Esa **cachonda** cojería cualquier cosa con piernas*
Literally, "bitch in heat."

Too bad he's an impotent.
*Qué lástima que es un **deficiente sexual**.*

That sterile dude couldn't get you pregnant with emotion.
*Ese **huevo duro** no te podría impregnar ni con el amor de Dios.*

Eww, you pervert!
*¡Bua, **perverso**!*

She keeps cheating on her cuckold of a husband.
*Ella le sigue engañando al **cornudo** de su marido.*
This is one of the most common and severe insults in Hispanic culture. It means you've been cheated on and made a fool of, and is frequently insinuated by making the devil horns sign with your hand and bumping it against your temple.

Stop making a cuckold of my brother!
*¡Basta de **ponerle los cuernos a** mi hermano!*

Careful, he's a ladies' man and a swinger to boot.
*Ojo, que es **un mujeriego** y en cima **un partusero**.*

He's always sleeping around.
*Siempre **anda culeando**.*

Quit humping my thigh, you **creep**.
*Basta de chocarme el muslo, **avión**.*

He may be cute, but that guy is a total **manwhore**.
*Está bien churro pero es un **perrote** total.*

That **cocksucker** cheated on me with my sister.
*Ese **mamavergas** me fue infiel con mi hermana.*

You'll never get your rocks off with that **dicktease**.
*Nunca vayas a echar un polvo con esa **calientapijas**.*

Your girlfriend is **frigid**.
*Tu novia es una **chuchafría**.* (Andes) | *...**coñofrío**.* (Spn)

That **easy slut**'s got a **quick-action pussy**.
*Esa **culopronto** tiene una **concha de lata**.*
Yes, *concha de lata* does mean "aluminum pussy." Why?
Because aluminum gets hot in seconds flat, that's why.

I wouldn't date **a loose girl** like her.
*Yo no me metería con **una flojona** como ella.* | *...**una
conchuda**...* (S.Cone)

I wouldn't fuck that hussy with *your* dick.
*A esa **zorra** no le metería ni la verga tuya.*

What a MILF!
*¡Que **MQTF**! (Spn)*
It's pronounced *Éme-quete-éfe* or *Mequete-éfe*, depending on whom you ask.

I tend to go for cougars.
*Yo suelo andar tras las **asaltacamas**.*

She looks like a virgin but I think she just plays innocent.
*Ella se parece **invicta** pero yo pienso que **se hace la inocente** nomás.*

They're just a big circle of fuckbuddies.
*Son un gran **enjambre mongol**.*
Literally, "Mongolian herd."

·····Jerking off
Pajas y pajeros

The most common and universal term for male masturbation, *paja*, is also the word for tumbleweed, which rolls around the plains in its eternal circular motion—poetic, huh? A *pajero*, then, can mean a drifter (like Don Quixote, for instance) who wanders aimlessly around the arid region; it could feasibly refer to a hay-monger; and in some places it means someone who babbles an endless stream of unimportant small talk (piling up the *paja*, as it were). But nine times out of ten, it means an excessive self-lover. In 1983, Mitsubishi even tried marketing an SUV to Latin America's quixotic drifter types under the name Pajero, but their dismal sales returns showed that no one wanted to drive around with "jack off" written on their car. Here are some less poetic synonyms if you want to avoid Mitsubishi's mix-up.

They call him the King of Jacks.
*A él le dicen **el Rey de la Paja**.*

He's a chronic wanker.
*Él es un **puñetero** mordaz.*

He never stops choking the chicken.
*Nunca se cansa de **pelársela**.*

He's always asking for help choking his chicken.
*Siempre pide ayuda **haciéndose una chaqueta**.* (Mex)

He was strokin' his salami like it was nothing.
***Se daba una manuela** como si nada.*

I get off on anal porn mostly.
*Tiendo a gozar de **porno anal**.*

I usually rub one out before I go to bed.
*Suelo **cascarme una pajita** antes de dormir.*

CHAPTER 6

ANGRY SPANISH
ESPAÑOL ENCABRONADO

Cursing in Hispanic cultures is a hugely popular, over-the-top form of poetry. Friends spar against each other like mortal enemies, gossips interrupt their narratives to unleash bucolic torrents of abuse on innocent passersby, and taxi drivers with little hope of a tip will spend five whole minutes roundly cursing a fellow driver. It's a way of life, a whole grammar of embellishment. Study up—or you might never fit in.

•••••Pissed off
Encabronado

Latins aren't more hot-blooded than other peoples, they're just more open and expressive about life's little murderous rages.

Fucking wetback beaners…
Frijoleros mojados…
Google the music video *Frijolero*, by Mexican rock supergroup Molotov, to get a feel for how offensive this term is.

Racist Republicans…
Republicanos migra…

Euro-mullets…
Esas melenas de gallego fofo (LatAm)… | Esas melenas de futbolista sudaca (Spn)…

   make me angry.
   me enojan.

   tick me off.
   me ponen del hígado.

   piss me off.
   me encabronan.

   get on my nerves.
   me ponen de los nervios.

   really bother me.
   me molestan seriamente.

   annoy the hell out of me.
   me fastidian hasta la madre.

You better not piss me off!
¡Mejor que no me chingues! (Mex)

Shut up!
¡Cállate!

Shut your trap!
¡Cierra el hocico!

You talk a lot of bullshit.
*Tú dices mucha **mierda**. | …**paja**.* (CenAm)

Get the hell away from me!
¡Pírate, carajo!

Get outta my face!
¡Lárgate de aquí!

I've fuckin' had it with you!
*¡Me tienes **harto**!*

Leave me alone.
Déjame en paz.

I'm about to lose my shit.
Estoy perdiendo mi puto quicio.

Keep **cussin' me out** and I'm gonna **snap** any second.
*Sigue **puteándome** y en cualquier momento voy a **soltar la rabia**.*

Somehow, "unleash the fury" (*soltar la rabia*) sounds less hokey in Spanish.

Go fuck yourself!
¡Vete a la mierda! | ¡Vete a la chingada! (Mex)

·····You talkin' to me?
¿A mí me lo dices?

What's your problem, man?
Pero, ¿qué te pasa?

What the fuck are you looking at?
¿Qué mierda miras así?

Stop frontin'!
¡No vaciles! (Spn) | *¡No bolacees!* (S.Cone)

What the hell is going on here?
¿Qué mierda está pasando por aquí?

SWEARING)))
PUTEANDO

Shucks!
¡Barajo! (Carib)

Shit!
¡Carajo!

Shitty!
¡Caray!

Darn!
¡Jolines! (Spn)

Damn!
¡Joder! (Spn)

Frick!
¡Pucha!

Fuck!
¡Puta!

Motherfucker!
¡A la gran puta!

What do you want, mother fucker?
¿Qué quieres, hijueputa?

What did you say to me?
¿Qué me dijiste?

Say that to my face, asshole!
¡Dímelo a la cara, pendejo!

·····Smack talk
Mentando madre

I can't stand that bitch!
¡No aguanto a esa puta!

She's such a gossip!
¡Qué chismosa!

He thinks he's the shit.
Él piensa que es la hostia. (Spn)

What a freak!
¡Qué frik! | ¡Qué friki! (Spn)

She's such a Debbie Downer.
¡Qué rebajón!

Did you see what she wore to the show last night?
¿Viste lo que tenía puesto anoche?

They're fake, definitely.
Seguro que son falsas.

I heard his dick is tiny.
Tengo oído que su verga es pequeñita.

OMG! Can you believe she actually showed up?
¡ALV (a la verga)! ¿Puedes creer que al fín vino?

Oh, hell no! He better not be talking shit about me!
¡Ni de coña! ¡Espero que no esté hablando pestes de mí! (Spn)

He is such a deadbeat.
Él es un haragán total.

Oh no she didn't! She did not just try to mac on Susie's boyfriend.
¡Nomedigas que ella acaba de tirar onda al novio de Susie!

·····Don't be stupid
No seas gil

The most basic and prolific Spanish insult is an attack on one's intelligence. Scholars suggest that Hispanics have so many words for stupidity because they have childlike minds and are insecure about their mental capacities. To that I say, "Takes one to know one, Mr. Smartypants Poopybreath!"

You're kinda stupid, aren't you?
Eres medio tontito/a, ¿no?

Were you born this slow, or did that just happen recently?
¿Naciste lento/a, o pasó recién?

The kid's got rocks for brains. He's totally out to lunch.
Este chico tiene piedras por sesos. Es totalmente lelo.

Don't be such a...
No seas...

He's/She's a complete...
Él/Ella es un...completo.

That fat American is a flat-out...
Ese/a yanqui gordo/a es un/una...pleno.

dummy
gil
You can dress this one up as *un flor de gil*, which translates to "a royal dumbass."

dumbass

gilún

When dumbasses travel in packs, you can refer to the herd as *una gilada*, or "a bunch of dumbasses."

dumbfuck

gilazo | gilipollas (Spn)

bag of rocks

maleta

doofus

buey

Literally, "ox."

blockhead

adoquín | cuadrado/a (S.Cone)

serious scatterbrain

pasmado/a

moron

mamerto/a | panoli (Spn)

SCORES OF WHORES)))
PUTEANDO A LAS PUTAS

Spanish has so many words for actual sex workers that, over time, half of them have become semi-benign terms used for slutty amateurs and ex-girlfriends you're not even mad at.

Bitch	*Puta*
Tramp	*Mujerzuela*
Skank	*Una macarra* (*un macarra* is a pimp!)
Slut	*Pelandusca	cuero* (Carib, Andes)
Ho	*Hortera	gata* (S.Cone)
Hoochie	*Una guarra	un yiro* (S.Cone)
Whore	*Zorra	jinetera* (Mex, Carib)
Hooker	*Fulana* (also means "random girl"), *Pendón* (Spn)
Trick	*Furcia	lumi* (Spn)
Prostitute	*Ramera	guaricha* (Andes)

nitwit / dimwit / halfwit
baboso/a ; atarantado/a ; tarado/a

retard
retardado/a

mental deficient
infradotado/a

Mongoloid
mogólico/a | oligofrénico/a (S.Cone)

·····Talkin' 'bout yo' mama
Mentándote la madre

When you're ready to take the confrontation out of first gear, try out one of the following aspersions on someone's character or heritage. They're guaranteed to bring on a case of what Spanish speakers call *mala sangre*. Remember to tuck your chin before you get punched in the face.

You're nothing but a…
No eres nada sino un/una…

You're no better than a two-bit, scummy…
Eres tan ruin, mezquino/a…

My cheating excuse for a husband is a real…
El canalla engañador de mi marido es un/una…de veras.

What a…!
¡Qué…!

sunnuvabitch
hijueputa ; 'jueputa

sunnbitch
joputas | juepuchas (S.Cone)

son of a royal old bitch
hijo de la gran puta vieja

creep
desgraciado/a

piece of trash
basura

motherfucker
conchesumá (S.Cone)
From *concha de su madre* ("his mother's cunt").

royal asshole
hijo de la gran po

bastard
guacho (S.Cone)

prick
carepicha (CenAm)
From *cara de picha* ("dick face").

cocksucker
chupapollas
Yes, this term connotes as much homophobia in Spanish as in English.

fucker
ojete

fuck-up
mamón

dipshit
mamila (Mex)

abomination
aborto
Literally, "abortion."

born asshole
malparido
Literally, "badly born" or "miscarriage that survived."

plague
peste

vermin
insecto

worm
larva

·····Go to hell
Véte al carajo

The purest Spanish curses tell their recipients to get lost, then offer an activity for them to do once they're gone. That activity usually involves being killed, anally penetrated, or covered in the vaginal secretions of their mother (you know, the usual).

Clear out! Scram!
¡Corta campo! ¡Rájate!

Go fly a kite.
Vete a espulgar un galgo.
Literally, "Go de-flea a greyhound."

Go to hell!
¡Ándate bien al carajo!

Go wipe your ass!
¡Anda a limpiarte el culo!

Go fuck yourself!
¡Cáchate! (Per)

Fuck you!
¡Chíngate! (Mex) | *¡Que te den!* (Spn)

Fuck off!
¡Andate a joder! (S.Cone)

Don't set foot in here again or I'll put you in a cast lickety-split.
No vuelves a poner pie aquí *o te lo pongo en un yeso rapidingo.*

Oh, **go spank your monkey,** you useless son of a bitch!
*¡Anda, **hazte una manuela**, hijueputa inútil!*

Go to hell and **put a finger in your ass** when you get there!
*¡Vete al diablo y **métete el dedo en el ojete** cuando llegues!*

Why don't **you go give yourself a good enema?**
*¿Por qué no **te vas a hacer una buen enema**?*

Why don't you take that billy club and **go fuck yourself with it?**
*¿Por qué no te llevas ese bolillo y **te lo metes en el culo**?*

Go try your bullshit on the hooker that spawned you!
*¡**Ándate a cantar tus pavadas** a la ramera que te parió!*

Go knock on the tired poontang of the hoochie you call a mom!
*¡**Rájate, que claves en la recalcada chocha** de la gata que llamas mami!*

Go to the rotten cunt of your whore mother!
*¡**Vete al coño podrido** de tu puta madre!*

·····Talkin' shit
Diciendo cagadas

Spanish speakers inherited the Roman obsession with poop, or specifically, the idea that a civilization should be judged by the sophistication of its plumbing. This is a big deal in Spanish since Latin Americans, as descendants of indigenous peoples, are *very* insecure about being considered "civilized." This is why the strongest cussword in Spanish is not "fuck" or "cunt," but "to shit." And the most dramatic form of shitting (and the mother of all Spanish insults) is to shit on one's enemies.

I shit on...!
¡Me cago en...!

my bitch-ass ex-boyfriend/girlfriend
mi re-que-te-jodido/a ex-novio/a

my old man and his stupid curfew
mi viejo y su queda idiota

my asshole of a boss
el huevón de mi jefe

crooked-ass Customs—let them fleece the next guy
la aduana chingona—que chinguen al próximo

the Host (of the Eucharist)
la hostia
This anti-Catholic expletive refers to the toiletbowl-like gesture made by the cupped hands of the priest administering the Eucharist.

the head of Benito Juárez
la cabeza de Benito Juárez
You might hear fervent Catholics uttering this one, as Benito Juárez is still detested in the God-fearing world for separating church and state.

my perverted **neighbor**
*mi **vecino** perverso*

the ridiculous toupee of Petey Wilson
el peluquín ridículo de Piti Wilson
Pete Wilson was formerly California's governor and chief supporter of Proposition 187, which stripped illegal immigrants of government services and basic human rights. He's still reviled among U.S. Latinos.

my idiot of a president
el idiota de mi presidente

your Mongoloid whore of a mother for having birthed you
la puta mogólica de tu mamá por haberte parido

your mother's torn-up, whoring cunt
el coño reventado de tu madre ramera
The H-bomb of all Spanish curses.

·····Fightin' words
Palabras peladas

The best part of any barfight is the moment just before fists start flying, when the two dudes are talking about all the nasty things they're going to do to each other and how hard they're gonna fuck each other up. It's so homoerotic that you're not sure if they're gonna fight each other or just gonna start fucking right there on the bar.

I'm gonna **kick your ass!**
*¡Te voy a **madrear!*** (Mex)

I'm gonna **tie you in knots.**
*Te voy a **atar en nudos**.*

Take it easy, I don't wanna have to **knock you to pieces.**
*Tómalo con calma, no quiero tener que **reventarte**.*

I'm gonna crack that hollow gourd of yours in half!
*¡**Te voy a partir** esa calabaza vacía!*

I'm gonna **open a can of whoop-ass** you won't soon forget!
*¡Te voy a **dar una paliza** de recuerdo!*

Keep givin' me the stinkeye and I'm gonna **make mincemeat** out of you!
*¡Sigue con la ojeriza y te voy a **hacer polvo**!*

He's gonna **whoop** me **like an eggbeater!**
*¡Me va a **batir como la crema para la torta**!*

I'm gonna **mop the floor with your hideous face,** you Mongoloid!
*¡Te voy a **usar la cara espantosa como trapo de piso**, mogólico!*

You're gonna get ripped to shreds!
¡Te va a dejar harapiento!

I'm gonna fuck you up royally!
¡Te voy a hacer una mierda líquida!
Literally, "I'm gonna make liquid shit out of you."

I'm gonna go medieval on your ass!
¡Voy a practicar el medioevo con tu culo!

Spread your cheeks cuz I'm 'bout to leave your asshole looking like the Holland Tunnel!
¡Ábrete las cachas porque estoy a punto de dejarte el ojete como el túnel de Holanda!

·····Punches and kicks
Golpes y patadas

The great thing about Spanish is the precision afforded by its suffixes, perhaps the coolest of which is *-azo*. When added to the end of a noun it basically means "the act of being smacked by (that noun)." So if your girlfriend throws dishes at you and lands one, it's *un platazo*, if you throw the cat right back at her it's *un gatazo*, if the wall crashes on her it's *un paredazo*, and so on.

Did you see that punch?
¿Viste ese puñetazo?

He smacked him good.
Le zumbó bien. | ...sonó... (Mex)

She broke his nose with that bitchslap.
Le rompió la nariz con ese cachetazo.

I'm gonna haul off and deck you if you don't shut your mouth.
Te voy a dar una paliza súbita si no te callas la boca.
La paliza súbita, "the sudden whoop-ass," can refer to a hurricane or just an unexpected and devastating swat to the back of the head, particularly from a parent.

Damn, you just **knocked him out** cold!
*¡Híjole, que **lo dejaste** frío!*

I **backhanded** that fool and gave him a **black eye**.
*A ese gilazo le dí **un sopapo trasero** y le dejé con un **ojo morado**.*

You **slap** like a girl.
*Das **guantazos** como una nena.*
Literally, "glove slaps," like for a duel.

I'm gonna **uppercut** your face.
*Te voy a **dar un ganchazo** en la cara.*

I'll **karate chop** you in the neck.
*Te voy a **dar un hachazo de karate** en el cuello.*

Kick him in the nuts!
*¡**Patéale** en los huevos!*

Put him in a **headlock**!
*¡Ponle en una **llave de cabeza**!*

Did you see that?! She picked him and **put him in a pile driver**!
*¿Viste eso? ¡Lo agarró y **le hizo el martinete**!*

I'll **kill** you, asshole!
*¡Te voy a **carnear**, pendejo!*

•••••Chill out
Cálmate

If you ever find yourself in a Latin American shantytown without a police squadron of protection, you may want to hide the shiny digital camera and start remembering some of these phrases.

Can't we all just **get along**?
*¿No podríamos **llevarnos bien** nomás?*

Quit it, boys, **break it up**.
*Basta, chicos, **déjenlo**.*

Take it outside.
Llévalo afuera.

Calm the fuck down!
¡Cálmense, carajo!

Dude, get a hold of yourself!
¡Contrólate, chavo!

Don't flip out!
!No flipes!

Slow down, tough guy.
Frénalo un poco, macho.

Get off it, man!
¡Déjelo, hombre!

Just forget about it.
Olvídalo nomás.

It's not worth it.
No vale la pena.

Let's all just take it easy.
Tomémoslo con calma.

I'm not looking for a fight.
No estoy buscando riña. | …buscando buya. (Carib)

Relax, I was just playin'.
Calma, era un chiste nomás.

Make love, not war.
Haz el amor, no la guerra.

Who wants a group hug?
¿Quién quiere un abrazo comunal?

CHAPTER 7

POPPY SPANISH
ESPAÑOL "POP"

Uncle Sam might like to think of everyone south of the border as a rustic farmhand sleeping against a cactus or lagging behind a *burro*, but Latin Americans are a lot more tech- and media-savvy than most of the Third World. Whether downloading bootleg DVDs, sending dirty text messages to a mistress, Skyping to friends abroad, or bumping tunes from an off-brand MP3 player, the Spanish speaker of the twenty-first century is a real media multitasker. So don't hold it against me if it takes you more than this chapter to catch up.

·····The TV
La tele

Television shows in Spanish are essentially the same as those in English, with two notable exceptions: more boobs and more crying. Whether you're tuned to news coverage, nature documentaries, police dramas, soap operas, game shows, or even cable-access shows about UFOs, you're pretty much guaranteed a public display of emotion and/or cleavage every 10 minutes, or your money back.

Keep channel surfing and I'm gonna shove the remote up your ass.
Sigue haciendo zapping y voy a meterte el remoto en el ojete.

What's on TV?
¿Qué hay en la tele?

TV SHOWS

Sábado Gigante

This kitschy hodgepodge of a game show, talk show, children's show, and sketch comedy was filmed live for eight straight hours every Saturday for 24 years in Chile—and in Miami for 21 years since. All that time, it's been synonymous with its charismatic host, "Don Francisco." All over Latin America and in the Latino U.S., Don Francisco is a household name whose show generally rates higher than any locally produced competition.

ShowMatch

Argentina's top-rated variety show continually morphs genres to hold down its spot in the rankings, phasing in and out new formats (mini-gameshows, sketch comedy miniseries, and so on). In between new ideas, though, they stick to classics, like getting comedian Yayo (Adam Sandler meets Howard Stern) to offend starlets with dirty jokes, and following the ensuing confrontations and offstage hissyfits with a handheld camera, Jerry Springer–style.

Los Conquistadores del Fin del Mundo

The survival reality subgenre has been huge in Latin America. The biggest of the bunch have been *Expedición Crusoe* (the same as our *Survivor*) and *Los Conquistadores del Fin del Mundo* (similar to *The Amazing Race*). Filmed in the Argentine Patagonia, contestants on *Conquistadores* race to the famous "End of the World Lighthouse" in Ushuaia. There's even an edition in which only pure-blooded Basques can compete!

Cantando/Bailando por un Sueño (Mexico and Argentina)

Like *Dancing with the Stars*, professional singers or dancers pair up with a celebrity of the opposite sex to sing or dance a duet. But since the Mexican version blew up the charts by substituting singing for dancing, Argentina had to up the ante and produce ice-skating with the stars. A musical-comedy version of *Cantando por…* is in the works, as well as a spin-off devoted to (I kid you not) competitive swimming.

Kassandra

This Venezuelan soap powerhouse about a gypsy marrying into money holds the Guinness record for most exported Spanish-language television show, with 128 countries having picked it up. During its bloody civil war, Serbia was one of these 128. Curiously, the daily cease-fire in Sarajevo coincided with the hour *Kassandra* aired. Coincidence?

Miramar

To Mexicans, *Miramar* was just another vendetta-filled *telenovela* about a working-class girl, her Prince Charming, and the backbiting bitches in the prince's family. But when it was broadcast during Ramadan of 1997, it caused such a sensation that a council of Muslim clerics in Abidjan, worried about the show's runaway popularity, actually rescheduled evening prayers to keep up mosque attendance!

Los Hombres de Paco

This cop-drama about a somewhat incompetent trio of idiot cops is currently Spain's top-rated fiction show, even though it has heapings of black-comedy and social commentary, two things notoriously absent from American prime time.

·····The movies
Las pelis

Usually, the names of American movies are given direct Spanish translations when they're released abroad. But the monolingual lackeys who slave away in studio think tanks occasionally decide on titles that make those online translation websites look graceful: *101 Dalmations* nonsensically became "Night of the Cold Noses," *Mrs. Doubtfire* turned into the saccharine "Your Daddy Forever," and *Brokeback Mountain* was given a title that I'm pretty sure was stolen from a Hardy Boys novel: "The Secret in the Mountain."

Let's go see a...on the big screen.
*Vámonos a ver un/una...**en pantalla grande**.*

How long has that...been running?
*¿Desde cuándo **está en cartel** ese/esa...?*

    tearjerker
    lacrimógena

    cartoon
    dibujo animado

    screwball comedy
    comedia blanca

    meathead movie
    película machote

    chick flick
    peli melosa

    feel-good hit of the year
    éxito sensacional de optimismo ligero

    documentary
    documental

    B movie
    película "serie B"

    porno
    porno

Is it dubbed? Cuz it's just not the same without Sean Connery's Scottish accent.
*¿Está **doblada**? Porque no es la misma cosa sin el acento escocés de Sean Connery.*

Who cares if it has subtitles? I can't read that fast.
*¿A quién le importa si tenga **subtítulos**? Yo no leo tan rápido.*

·····Comics
Los cómics

Comics are *huge* in the Spanish-speaking world—people of all walks of life read cheap comics in a whole range of genres that we simply don't have here. Granny flips through her B&W soap-operas, Gramps mutters into his bound anthology of yesteryear's political cartoons, the goth kid next to you chuckles into his true-crime slasher, the hormone-case across the aisle isn't trying hard enough to hide the boner his girly comic is giving him. Even the pamphlets that Jehovah's Witnesses put in your hand are surprisingly stylish bits of comic art!

In Latin America in particular, they're still a major art form and mass media entertainment. Here are some landmarks from the golden age of comics right up to the present.

Memín Pinguín
(México: 1940s, 372 issues, continuously in print/reprint ever since)

Mafalda
(Argentina: 1964–1973) Far more subtle (and often overtly political)

Condorito
(Chile: 1955–1985) Less political and intellectual than Mafalda (and thus, continuously published for over 40 years)

Supercholo
(Perú: 1955–1966; 1994–1998)

Mortadelo & Filemón
(Spain: 1955–present)

Los Agachados
(Mexico: 1968–1981)

Revista Fierro
(Argentina: 1984–1992; 2006–present)

Where are your…?
¿Dónde tiene usted las…?

Are this week's…in?
¿Ya tienes las…de está semana?

>**comic strips (typically sold in anthologies)**
>*tiras cómicas*
>
>**political cartoons (single-frame political comics)**
>*viñetas políticas*
>
>**comic books**
>*historietas | tebeos* (Spn) | *moneros* (Mex)
>
>**soap opera comics**
>*comics sentimentales*
>
>**kids' comics**
>*comics infantiles*
>
>**Japanese comics**
>*comics manga* (never conjugated)

·····Pop music
Música "pop"

Pop music and ghetto music have been all but synonymous in Latin America since long before gangster rap turned suburban malls into a carnival of white-kid posturing. These are the hotter currents in Spanish-speaking pop music nowadays, for better or for worse.

Let's listen to some…
Ponnos algo de…

Bump that…
Súbele a esa…

I can't stand…
No soporto…

Norteñas

Norteñas are border songs, ballads about *coyotes* (people-smugglers) and *narqueros* (drug-smugglers) set to an evolved *Banda* (border-country) tune that's lighter on the polka backbeat. Imagine Garth Brooks doing uptempo, happy-dance covers of gangster-rap songs with an accordion.

Cumbia

This term refers to a whole family of pop genres including everything from saccharine singalongs to Timberlakey pop to dance-party jams, all featuring an Andean blend of catchy hooks; solid, danceable backbeats; and melodies even a drunk could follow. The lyrics tend to be salt-of-the-earth, the instrumentation jangly and keyboardy, and the clubs where it's DJ'ed insipid and Budweiser-esque. But even at its worst, *cumbia* is like a good wedding band: functional for everyone, irritating to no one.

Reggaetón

Around the time Shaggy and Sean Paul were bringing Jamaican "Dancehall" to the U.S., pop stars like Tego Calderón, Don Omar, and Calle 13 (think Jay-Z, 50 Cent, and Ludacris, respectively) started adapting the genre to the palates of Latin American listeners. The production is less smoked-out than its Jamaican cousin, with lyrics closer to top-40 hip-hop than gangsta rap or Jamaica's terrifying fagbash subgenre.

Perreo

This Puerto Rican predecessor to *Reggaetón* has all but disappeared into the dustbin of pop music history. However, the name ("doggy-business") is still used to refer to hardcore bumping and grinding or *sexo vestido* ("sex with clothing on").

Funk Carioca (aka Baile funk)

What's not to love about hypnotically simple, early hip-hop and late funk beats, and remarkably crude lyrics about car stereos and big asses? Younger readers more familiar with Crunk and Baltimore House might find it too hokey and cheerful, but *funk carioca* is really a revival of Miami Bass, where all that dirty south shit got started.

Ibiza

Thanks to mammoth dance clubs like Manumission (capacity 10,000) and various electronic-music festivals, this resort island in Baleares, Spain has long rivaled Berlin as the epicenter of Europe's dance club culture. Its name, when used as an adjective, refers to boiled-down, slightly sleazy house music somewhere between vintage Detroit House and a car-commercial version of Acid House.

Salsa

Outside of a few specific places, *Salsa* is as dorky and pony-tailed as it is in suburban America, no matter how short the skirts, how high the heels, or how slutty the afterparties. I'm only including this among real pop genres to discourage some persistent rumors to the contrary.

Don't laugh, but I'm secretly a huge fan of Juanes.
No te ries, pero soy un fan de Juanes.

I heart Charly García! I even like his recent CDs.
Amo a Charly García! Hasta me gustan los nuevos discos.

What's your favorite band?
¿Cúal es tu banda?

I heard El Guincho is playing a gig at a bar tonight.
*Tengo oído que El Guincho va a **tocar un bolo** en un bar a la noche.*

I really like the chorus of this song.
Me encanta el coro de está canción.

·····Computer-ese
Jerga informática

Like anywhere else in the world, most techie lingo is just barely transliterated English. But for the sake of teaching by example, here are the less obvious basic terms. If you really want to learn computer-ese, though, set the language to Spanish on your OS, your cell phone, and your software, and then teach yourself the hard way.

Does your apartment have broadband?
*¿Tu departamento tiene **banda ancha**?*
Cable predominates over DSL most everywhere, but both are usually called *banda ancha*.

POKEMONESe)))
POKE-EMO

If you thought 'leet-speak was annoying (4nd wh0 d035nt?), wait till you see what horrible monstrosities have been unleashed on the Spanish language by Latin America's geeky obsession with Pokemon.

> ***Kieeh beiioÓóoòòòh*** *(¡qué bello!)*
> How pretty!
>
> ***t0 R sHhuLoNaÀhh*** *(¡Está re-culona!)*
> She's got hella booty!
>
> ***illoooooo ame un leru!!*** *(¡'Elooo, dame un euro!)*
> Heeeey, gimme a buck!

There's a movie I've been trying to compress and upload to you on Limewire.
*Hay una peli que vengo tratando de comprimir y **subir** por Limewire.*

Just as *subir* means "to upload," *bajar* means "to download."

My home machine's totally fucked.
*Mi **compu de casa** está jodida.*

E-mail it to me as an attachment so I can print it out.
Mándamelo *como **archivo adjunto** para que lo pueda **imprimir**.*

Where'd you get that DVD that plays bootlegs and DivX movies?
*¿Dónde conseguiste ese DVD que toca los **piratas** y los **DivX**?*

Thanks to tiny SRT subtitle files that are legal to up- and download, international video piracy is now as easy as ripping the subtitle track off an American DVD. This allows Spanish-subtitled DivX files to appear months before the official DVD releases, and makes it easy for anime freaks to translate everything the studios don't.

Do I need a **password** to access your USB **pendrive**?
*¿Necesito **contraseña** para acceder tu **llavero** USB?*

What's your **login**?
*¿Cúal es tu **nombre de usario**?*

Are you **online**?
*¿Estás **en linea**?*

Check out my **website**.
*Mira a mi **sitio web**.*

I posted a link **on your wall**.
*Puse un enlace **en tu muro**.*

Friend me on Facebook.
***Agrégame** en Facebook.*

Your profile pic is hilarious!
¡Tu foto de perfil está rebuena!

What do you use for a nick?
¿Qué usas como handle?

It really blows my mind the things rappers tweet about.
Me vuela la cabeza las cosas que twittean los rappers.

My **off-brand player** holds twice as many MP3s as your **iPod**!
*¡Mi **reproductor de cuarta** guarda dos veces los MP3s que tu **iPod**!*

That **backdrop** is a little inappropriate, don't ya think?
*Ese **papel tapiz** es poco apropiado, ¿no te parece?*

Fifteen minutes of **Googling** and the damn **Wikipedia** doesn't qualify as "research."
*Quince minutos de **Googlear** y el pinche **Wiki** no cualifica como "investigación."*

The **link** you sent me took me to **tranny porn**!
*¡El **enlace** que me mandaste me llevó a **porno trave**!*

·····Text messaging
SMSeando

Text messaging is *huge* in Spanish-speaking lands—largely because neither Spaniards nor Latin Americans can afford to talk on the phone much, given the ruthless price-fixing and gouging of their telecom markets. Unfortunately for non-native speakers, spry youngsters keep raising the bar on cryptic abbreviations and acronyms.

I love you always	tq 100pre	*(te quiero siempre)*
What	q	*(que)*
Where	dde	*(donde)*
Here	ak	*(aquí)*
Because	xq	*(porque)*
I don't know	nc	*(no sé)*
No	–	*(no)*
Bye	xau	*(ciao)*
Hope you're well	ke tii bn/ktbn	*(que estés bien)*
Idiot	won	*(huevón)*
Shit	mela	*(mierda)*
I shit on you	tkg	*(te cagué)*
Suck it	xupalo	*(chúpalo)*
Your mother's pussy	ctm	*(chocha ; concha ; coño de tu madre)*

T kiero + q tdo l mndo, toy :D
Te quiero más que todo el mundo, estoy contento.
I love you more than all the world, I'm so happy.

M da =, won
Me da igual, huevón
It's the same to me, moron.

Uds fue a s bar nue? Dde qda?
¿Ustedes fueron a ese bar nuevo? ¿Dónde queda?
Did you guys go to that new bar? Where is it?

Qan2 m aqerde t qnto. Sta nfrmø tdv?
Cuando me acuerde te cuento. ¿Estás enfermo todavía?
I'll tell you when I remember. Are you still sick?

Stoi bn pro tmpko mxo mjor tqG
Estoy bien, pero tampoco mucho mejor. Te quiero, G.
I'm better, but not much better, either. Love, G.

·····Fashion
La moda

Although, or maybe because, half the world's sweatshops and *maquilladoras* are in Latin America, big-city Spanish speakers can be as shallow and ruthless as any of those catty amateurs on *Project Runway*. Here are some basics for clawing and hissing.

The Twiggy look is totally in vogue—quit eating now!
*El estilo Twiggy está muy **en boga**—¡basta de comer, ya!*

That dress…
Ese vestido…

> **is so cute.**
> *está divino.*
>
> **is so trashy.**
> *es callejero.*
>
> **is so skanky.**
> *es de hortera.* (Spn)
>
> **is so last season.**
> *está pasado de temporada.*
>
> **is so unflattering.**
> *es poco favorecedor.*

Is that vintage?
*Eso es **vintage**?*

Wearing a sports jersey to a funeral is pretty tacky.
*Ir a un entierro de camiseta deportiva es bien **chabacano**.*

Take off that beret, you look like a **yuppie** in midlife crisis!

*¡Quítate esa boina, pareces un **yuppie** en crisis de edad!*

Her **hipster** vibe is so fake. Her tattoos aren't even real!

*Su aire de **modernilla** es tan falso. ¡Falsos aún los tatuajes!* (Spn) | *…**cheta**…* (S.Cone)

I pretend I'm not into all that **bling-bling**, but when I see platinum and ice like that….

*Disimulo cualquier interés en el **blinblineo**, pero cuando veo a platino y hielo así….*

Faux snakeskin is really **trendy** right now.

*La piel de serpiente falsa está bien **de moda** al momento.*

I think the Louis Vuitton bag my boyfriend got me is **fake**!

*Me parere que la bolsa Louis Vuitton que me regaló mi novi es **falsa**!* | *…**trucha**!* (S.Cone)

·····Youth cultures
Tribus urbanas

Los rockeros

Rock has a totally different meaning in every Hispanic culture. In Mexico, the boundaries between black metal, stoner metal, punk, industrial, and butt-rock are pretty permeable, making anyone who likes any of the above a *rockero*. In Argentina, *rockeros* are specifically aficionados of *rock nacional*, as opposed to the imported stuff (mostly American) hogging the airwaves. So sporting a U2 shirt makes you a *rockero* in Mexico but a sell-out in Argentina.

Aggros

In Nu Metal–crazed Chile, *los aggros* issued an ultimatum to *los rockeros*: Jettison your attachment to all rock subgenres that came before Nu Metal, throw out your Rolling Stones records, and stop washing your hair, or else we won't let you into our Worlds of Warcraft clan! Unfortunately, large numbers of the *huevones* took them up on it.

Los punkeros (aka ponkeros)

The robust tradition of anarchism in Spain trickled down to Latin America when Spanish anarchists fled there after the Spanish Civil War, turning anarchy into a real way of life rather than just a fashion statement, as it was in the U.K. Latin American punks are therefore a little more rebellious than their Anglo counterparts, less likely to get a job, and more likely to end up making pipe bombs than just silk-screening edgy slogans onto patches.

Los marquitos

Subcomandante Marcos, leader of the Zapatista movement, maintains semianonymity to this day. After those massive "we are all Marcos" rallies where flash-mobs would don the Zapatista ski-mask "uniform," would-be Marcoses became affectionately known as *Marquitos*. But this pet name is slowly becoming reserved for middle-class poseurs who sport Che Guevara shirts and mall-bought Mayan man-purses, and who use their English tutors to translate Rage Against the Machine lyrics.

Los "darks" (aka moribundos, góticos)

Goths are different in the Hispanic world, mostly because black lace is more grandma than edgy, and fake blood is a bit mundane after all the civil wars and the weekly "blood-drinking" at Mass. Hispanic goths are more into serial killers, sadomasochism, politics, and banned horror films than Victorian kitsch, burlesque, and séances. And they prefer to make their own clothes rather than shop at Hot Topic.

Los bakalas ; Los bakaleros

Once slang for "fresh," as in "fresh as Bilbao *bacalao* (cod)," this term then came to refer nostalgically to the golden age of Spanish dance club culture. Nowadays, though, Spaniards use the word to refer derogatorily to MDMA burnouts and tacky 16-year-olds bumpin' goa-trance in their lowered Hondas.

Los emos (aka sensibles)

Yup, same as at your high school—the sensitive kids wear sweaters and Converse All-Stars. They like sappy screamo and they slouch a lot. Their doting moms probably sewed those precious little homemade patches onto their Jansports for them. Recently, Mexican emos have borne the brunt of nationwide mob violence at the hands of *punkeros* and *rockeros* who are sick of them "biting their style." (No, really—emos are getting the shit kicked out of them in bloody riots over who pierced what first!)

Los niños bien, aka el chetaje (S.Cone), los yeyés (Pan), los pijos (Spn)

Yes, even the poorest corners of Spain and Latin America boast a robust leisure class, and each country has its own name for the bunch. This group tends more to the overtanned-Eurotrash, stone-washed-jeans look than the American country club preppy set.

Los poperos (aka poppis)

Want to stick out with a glossy subcultural persona without all the conflict of being anti-anything? Why not join the rank and file of the pretty boys and baby dolls who can't think of anything better to identify with than asinine Shakira-style pop music! It's "hurrah for everything" every day for these perky little bottles of Prozac.

SPORTY SPANISH
ESPAÑOL DEPORTISTA

·····Soccer
Fútbol

Wherever Spanish is spoken, there is only one sport—football. Not the kind with quarterbacks and piles of sweaty men gangbanging each other on the field with nickel defenses, but the *real* kind: *fútbol*. Many of the key terms used to talk about football are easy enough for an English speaker to pick up because, well, they're English words, including that monosyllabic word that sports announcers belt out for 90 seconds at a time.

Who's your favorite…?
¿Cuál es tu…favorito?

I wanna kill that…!
¡Quiero matar a ese…!

That…is legit.
*Es **chévere** ese…* (Mex, Carib) | *…**bárbaro**…* (S.Cone, Andes)

That...sucks.
Es una mierda ese...

> **team**
> *equipo*

> **franchise**
> *club*

> **forward**
> *delantero/a*
> This is the guy who scores all the goals, takes his shirt off, and goes running around the field with his arms out like an airplane.

> **defender**
> *defensa*
> This is one of the guys who plays in back and has thighs like tree trunks.

> **sweeper**
> *líbero/a*
> This guy is the last line of defense between the defensive line and the goalie.

> **goalie**
> *portero/a | golero/a* (Mex)
> If you don't know what a goalie is, you probably shouldn't even be reading this book.

> **coach**
> *entrenador/a*

> **referee**
> *árbitro/a*

How do I get to the stadium/court?
¿Cómo llego a la cancha?

Come on, let's see how cheap tickets are from that scalper.
Vámonos, a ver como están de baratas las entradas de ese revendedor/a.

Wanna grab a beer at halftime?
¿Quieres conseguir una cerveza entre medios?

Number 9 scored a hell of a goal.
El nueve metió un golazo.

What's the score?
*¿Y el **tanteo**?*

Their team scored two goals.
*Su equipo **marcó** dos goles.*

Goooooooooaaaaaaaaallllllllllllllllllllllllllllllllllllllllllllll!
¡Goooooooooooooooooooooolllllllllllllllllllllllllll!
The *gooooooooooooooool*-yelling tradition, which seems so timeless, was actually limited to Argentine radio and TV until the 1990 World Cup, when an Argentine (and Boca-loyal) sportscaster, Andrés Cantor, set the standard by which all future sportscasters would be measured. Like opera singing, it's all in the diaphragm muscle.

·····For the fans
Para los hinchas

Who do you root for?
*¿A quién **apoyas**?* | *¿Por quién **hinchas**?* (S.Cone)

I'm a fan of Boca.
Soy hincha de *Boca.*
Hincha is a term used only for soccer fans. For all other sports, fans are either *fanáticos* or *aficionados*.

I'm a fan of Real Madrid.
*Soy **un forofo** de Real Madrid.* (Spn)

You're one of those hardcore, crazy fans, aren't you?
*Tú eres uno de esos **ultras**, ¿no?*
Ultra as in *ultrafanático*, the chest-painting kind.

I'm not a hooligan or anything like that. (the violent, rioting kind)
*No, **gamberro** no soy, ni nada al estilo.*

That blind fuckin' ref doesn't see anything!
*¡Ese **silbante** ciego de mierda no ve nada!*
Literally, "whistleblower."

Oh, come on, he shouldn't have called that!
¡Pero por favor, no debe haberlo pitado!
Careful: *Pitar* literally means "to blow a whistle," so it only refers to whistle calls.

Did the referee really just give him a yellow card for that?
*¿En serio, el árbitro le dió **una tarjeta amarilla** por eso?*

I'd have given him a red for it.
*Yo lo hubiera dado **una roja**.*

Foul!
¡Falta!

It looks like he took a good foul just to thwart the forward's rush.
*Parece que fue **una falta táctica** para detener el avance del delantero.*

I can barely hear you, everyone's cheering so loud!
*¡Apenas te oigo, todos están **alentando tan fuerte**!*

Look at the other team's supporters! They're gonna cry any minute!
*¡Mira **la barra** del otro club! ¡Se van echar a llorar!*

We are the champions!
*¡Somos **los/las campeones/as**!*

KNOCK-DOWN, DRAG-OUT RIVALRIES>>>
RIVALIDADES A BRAZO PARTIDO

You can't have a team without a rival team. And you can't have a rivalry without a major annual showdown that divides the country in half.

Mexican League: Guadalajara vs. Club América
Guadalajarans think of Mexico City as full of wannabe Europeans. Residents of Mexico City consider Guadalajara to be the backward epicenter of country music, working-class culture, and all things rural and "old school." Guada's team, *los chivos*, almost never drafts a player born outside of Mexico. Club América's team, *las aguilas*, has a roster full of ringers poached from the international circuit and European leagues. The match between these two teams restages the major political struggle of Mexican history, as evidenced in their nicknames: *los capitalinos y los provincianos*, or the Capital City kids and the Backwoodsmen.

Argentine League: Boca vs. River
These two Buenos Aires teams have been the major Argentine clubs for over a century. Boca, the name taken from the warehouse neighborhood at the mouth (*boca*) of the River Plata, are working-class heroes who've adopted the nickname *bosteros*, "manure shovelers." River, based among the English-speaking, country-club elites on the North (i.e., river) side of the city, is nicknamed *los millionarios*. The annual *superclásico* is such a spectator event that travel agencies sell package deals structured around it. But bring your riot gear! The mythology surrounding the teams sometimes turns the postgame riot into all-out class warfare.

Spanish League: Barcelona vs. Real Madrid
The two biggest, most successful teams in Spain face off twice a year, pitting the two major cities of the country and the two poles of Spanish life: Castilian civility vs. Cataluñian anarchy, standard Spanish vs. Catalán, and mainstream politics vs. separatist solidarity. Team Barcelona, nicknamed Barça, is called the *culers* or *culés*, because their popularity outgrew their tiny stadium in the '20s when anyone walking by saw the *culos* of the last fans to arrive hanging over the stadium wall. Team Madrid, made up of pretty boys in white uniforms, gets called *los merengues* and sports a prominent royal crown on its team crest—which might handicap its popularity if only they weren't so amazingly good (they hold the record for most European Cup titles).

·····"He's on fire!"
"¡Está que le sale!"

Half the fun of sports is the whole panoply of specialized cursing and poetic imagery that goes with it. Here are some basics to help get you started on the long road to decoding the banter of play-by-play announcers and SportsCenter repeats.

They're really **showing some hustle!**
*¡Se están **poniendo las pilas**!*
Literally, "putting in their batteries."

He's on a helluva **streak!**
*¡Esta en una buena **racha**!*

Get your fat ass in gear!
¡Muévete las nalgas anchas!

Get aross the field, already!
*¡Dale, **corta campo**!*

That referee is **blind as a bat!**
*¡Ese árbitro es un **murciélago**!*

Their defense is **pudding.**
*Su defensa es **un flan**.*

That defender's a real **pushover.**
*Ese defensa es un **queso** total.*

That forward **is stiff as a cast.**
*Ese delantero **es de yeso**.*

Check out **leadfoot** over there.
*Mira al **patadura** ese.*

He's total **deadweight.**
*Él es un **muerto** total.*

What an **oaf!**
*¡Qué **zafio/a**! | ...**croto**! (S.Cone)*

Stop being such a crybaby!
*¡Basta de hacerte el/la **llorón/as**!*

You call that offense, you pussyfooting dandy?
*¿Así juegas ofensa, **pechofrío remilgado**?*

They totally demolished us.
*Nos **dieron masa**.*
This actually means "they fucked us"—sports are as homoerotic in Spanish as in any language.

Did you see that lob? How the hell did he make the nationals?
*¿Viste a esa **masita**? ¿Cómo carajo llegó **a la [liga] nacional**?*

They're really putting up a fight!
*¡Mira si están **dándoles lucha**!*

It's gonna be a fight to the bloody end, fellas!
*¡Será **una lucha sin cuartel**, muchachos!*

·····For the players
Para los jugadores

Like in any other language, the set of words you need to yell at a television screen or all over the neck of the guy in front you is totally different from the vocabulary you'll need playing a pickup game in the park without getting sent back to the bench.

We don't need to form a league or anything, let's just kick the ball around.
*No necesitamos formar liga y todo, juguémonos un **partidillo** nomás. | ...un **picadito**...* (S.Cone)

Where can I play a pickup game around here?
*¿Dónde podría jugarme una **pachanga** por aquí? | ...una **caimanera**...* (Ven)
Note: Without the clarifying verb, people might think you mean the other use of the term *pachanga*: a swingin' party!

Pass it, he's open!
*¡Pásalo a él, que está **abierto**!*

Pass it here! I'm wide open!
*¡Pásalo por aquí! ¡Estoy **solo**!*

Soccer play terms:

Clear the ball!
¡Patee por adelante!
It's also common in everyday speech to use this phrase as a metaphor for short-term crisis management, like the American "putting out fires."

Header
Una cabecita

To dribble
Gambatear ; Regatear

Quick pass
Lanzar | Chutar (Mex)
From the English, "Shoot!"

Delayed pass
Un pase retrasado ; Una retrasada

Chip pass
Una vaselina corta

Lob
Una vaselina larga

Banana shot
Una vaselina curva
If you don't know what this means, look it up on YouTube.

Breakaway
Una internada

Bicycle kick
Una chilena

Nutmeg (to pass through the legs of the guy covering you)
Un túnel | Un caño (S.Cone) | *Una cacha* (Spn) | *Un huevo* (Par)

Hop (as in, pop over the head of the guy covering you)
Jopear (S.Cone)

·····Second-rate sports
Deportes de segunda

In most Spanish-speaking lands, anything but *fútbol* isn't really on the level of a "major sport." And if Spain weren't part of Europe, tennis and fencing and all those other fancy-boy sports wouldn't even be tolerated. So if you go asking around for a baseball diamond and get only blank stares, it's not because you're using the wrong word—it's because you're in the wrong place.

I play…
Yo juega al/a la…

I do…
Yo hago el/la…

Wanna go play some…?
¿Quieres ir a jugar…?

Is there any…on TV?
¿Hay…en la tele?

> **boxing**
> *boxeo*
>
> **racquetball**
> *squash*
> Technically, squash isn't racquetball, but people will be more likely to know what you're talking about if you ask them where you can play "squash."
>
> **basketball**
> *baloncesto*
>
> **tennis**
> *tenis*
>
> **fencing**
> *esgrima*
>
> **baseball**
> *béisbol*
>
> **swimming**
> *natación*

ViDƏO GAMƏS)))
VIDEOJUEGOS

Although kids in Latin America are crazy about video games, the process of getting adults to buy and play Wiis and Xboxes has been much harder to get going. The resistance to video games as "kid's stuff" is so deeply entrenched that many grown men with shrines to soccer heroes in their garages would slap me for even including this section in a chapter on sports.

Do you like playing video games?
¿Te gusta jugar videojuegos?

Know any good cheat codes for this game?
¿Conóces a algún código truco para este juego? [S.Am]

I've been stuck on this level for 21 hours.
Hace 21 horas que estoy en este nivel.

You just got totally owned.
Te acaban de ownear del todo.

He's not a novice, he's a total newb.
No es un novato, us un nuevón total.

surfing
el surf ; el surfo ; surfear
Like most borrowed words, there isn't really a stable, accepted form for "surfing." Young people are more likely to use the more "Spanicized" forms, and in more formal contexts people leave the English word in its original.

gymnastics
gimnasia

skiing
esqui

snowboarding
snowboard

karate
karate

pro wrestling
lucha libre

ultimate fighting
lucha hardcore

Careful, I'm a
black belt.
Cuídate, que soy
cinturón negro.

I can **break boards**
with my head.
*Puedo **romper***
***tablas** con la cabeza.*

Cheerleading is
too a sport!
*¡Sí, que **porrismo** es*
un deporte!

He blasted that **home
run**.
*Lanzó ese **jonrón**.*

It's going, going, gone! That's a **roundtripper**!
*¡Se va, se va, y se fué! ¡Es un **cuadrangular**!*

Did you see that **slam dunk**?
*¿Viste ese **clavado**?*

·····Other sports
Otros deportes

Uruguayans kick ass at…
Los uruguayos son fenomenales en…

Colombians can't play…for shit.
Los colombianos jugando…son una mierda.

Polo

Polo still looms big at the country-club end of the sports
spectrum in Latin America. Since the Latin- and Anglo-
American championships merged in 1987, Argentina and
Brazil have won all but one title, with Chile and Mexico helping
to keep America, England, and Australia out of the top three
(except for one blip in 1995). According to urban myth, polo

aficionado Sylvester Stallone owns over one quarter of the grassy Argentine province of Rio Negro, where he makes a killing raising world-class polo horses.

Kayak-polo

Yes, it's what you're thinking, and Spain has two televised competitive leagues of it.

Cesta-punta

This Basque variant of *jai alai* holds the Guinness world record for manually propelled ball speed: In 1979 someone threw a *pelota* out of a cyborg-looking basket-mitt at 188 mph! Rubber balls flung at that speed will break any bone they hit if you get between the thrower and the wall.

Pok-ta-pok

This Olmecan sport makes rugby look like a tea party. Each team has to somehow get a heavy, hemorrhage-inducing leather ball across an H-shaped court and through a hoop it barely fits in without using their hands or feet (tip: it's all in the elbows). The sport is played by Mayan-speaking communities throughout Southern Mexico and Guatemala. A few teams toured Germany in 2006, trying to stir up international interest in the sport. Maybe they need to bring back the human-sacrifice component to get over the low-scoring doldrums.

Lacrosse

Argentina and Spain both hold national championships and send teams to the world championships. Although they may not be able to hold their own against the American, Canadian, and Iroquois teams when they get there, they are heroes back home for even qualifying.

Rugby

Another tooth-loosener that Argies and Spaniards really get behind is rugby, that sport with all the man-hugging, dog-piling, and fabulous stripey shirts. If it didn't involve so much facial scarring, it could almost be considered fruity.

Béisbol

It's no coincidence that some of the best Major League Baseball players come from the Caribbean. Baseball is huge in Puerto Rico, the Dominican Republic, and Cuba. Outside the Caribbean, though, don't expect to find anyone who wants to trade cards with you.

Lucha Libre

Mexico's *luchas libres* are just as fake and theatrical as any WWF event, but the Mexican theatrical flair really comes out in the populist speeches the fighters deliver…*and* the vicious grandmothers in the audience screaming for blood.

•••••Other activities
Otras actividades

I'm way into…
Estoy muy metido en lo de…

> **yoga.**
> *el yoga.*
>
> **backpacking.**
> *el "trekking."*
>
> **hiking.**
> *el senderismo.*
>
> **road biking.**
> *el bicicletismo.*
>
> **jogging.**
> *el "footing."*
>
> **darts.**
> *los dardos.*
>
> **foosball / table football.**
> *el futbolín / el metegol.*
>
> **pool.**
> *el billar.*
>
> **Ping-Pong.**
> *el ping pong.*
>
> **dominoes.**
> *el dominó.*
>
> *Dominó* is more popular in the Caribbean than in just about any other part of the world; it's pretty easy to find a pickup game anywhere there, but also in Caribbean neighborhoods of Spain, Mexico City, Miami, and Nueva York. Just be careful they don't get the shirt off your back—it's a betting game, there more than here. Also note that in almost every country of the Caribbean, the rules are a little different—see the Spanish-language Wikipedia for an overview and links.

betting / gambling.
la timba.

bowling.
bolos ; bowling.
Bolos can refer to Ameican bowling or English bowls (aka *petanque*, bocci ball, etc.) For this reason, people increasingly use the English word to be more specific. *Un boliche* is the word for bowling alley in Mexico, but be careful when asking for directions to the nearest bowling alley in South America, where a *boliche* is a bar and a *bolin* ("bowling" pronounced quickly) is a brothel.

·····Working out
Haciendo ejercicios

Not into the whole team-sports thing? Prefer sweating in a room full of mirrors with tacky '80s music blaring and perverts pretending not to stare at you? Lucky for you, gym culture has caught on everywhere. Nowadays, you can even find gyms in places that barely have running water.

Where is/are…?
¿Dónde queda/quedan…?

the treadmill
las trotadoras | la caminadoras (Mex) | *la cintas de correr* (Spn)

the stair machine
la escaladora

the exercise bike
la bicicleta estacionaria

the freeweights
los pesas libres

the bench press
la banca

the pool
la piscina | la pileta (S.Cone) | *la alberca* (Mex)

I just did 1000…
Acabo de hacer mil…

push-ups.
las flexiones. | *las lagartijas.* (Mex)
Lagartijas literally means "lizards," which makes sense, since lizards are always kinda bobbing up and down on their arms.

pull-ups.
las dominadas.

sit-ups.
los abdominales. ; las sentadillas.

You're looking **ripped**!
*¡Te ves **macizo/a**!*

He must **work out**.
*Debe **entrenarse**.*

First, I'm gonna **stretch**.
*Primero, voy a **desperezarme**. ; ...**estirarme**.*

Wanna **go for a jog**?
*¿Quieres **salir a correr**?* | *...**a trotar**?* (Mex)

I'm **out of breath, sore, and need a cigarette desperately**.
*Estoy **sin aliento, adolorido, y necesito un cigarrillo desesperadamente**.*

CHAPTER 9

HUNGRY SPANISH
CASTELLANO HAMBRIENTO

Spanish speakers aren't pretentious or finicky about their food. They like honest fare cooked home-style, just the way *Mamá* made it. And they like to see their food being made—precooked food is considered an abomination in most places.

·····Hunger
Hambre

I'm starving.
Estoy hambriento/a.

I'm dying.
Me estoy muriendo.

I'm fucking hungry.
Estoy re-mal de filo.

Let's get some…
Vamos a conseguirnos algo de…

> **food.**
> *comida.*
>
> **eats.**
> *manduca.*

junk food.
comida basura. | *comida chatarra.* (LatAm)

fast food.
comida rápida. | *minutas.* (S.Cone)

street food.
garnacha. (Mex)

ethnic food.
comida étnica.

Let's grab a quick bite to eat.
¿Comemos algo rápido por ahí?

I just want a snack.
Sólo quiero un bocadito. | *...un piscolabis.* (Spn)

I want to stuff my face.
Quiero ponerme morado. (Spn)

Damn you just inhaled those sopes!
¡Carajo, acabas de inhalar esos sopes!

I'm craving...
Tengo antojo de...

> **barbecue.**
> *barbacoa.* (Mex) | *asado.* (S.Cone)
> Did you know we get the English word "barbecue" from
> the Spanish, which gets it from the Arawakan language
> indigenous to Haiti and the Dominican Republic? They didn't
> have iron, but they still managed to get their meat slow-
> roasted on a *barbakoa*, or "framework of sticks."

> **Italian food.**
> *comida italiana.*
> Luckily for you, Italians immigrated en masse to Latin America
> during the same period they were flooding America's East
> Coast cities, setting up those amazing delicatessens in some
> nook or cranny of every sizable Latin American city. Pizza may
> get kind of dodgy outside of the Southern Cone and Brazil,
> but in any Spanish-speaking city, a good mortadella sandwich
> or a plate of olivey pasta isn't hard to find.

chop suey/stir-fry.
chaufa.
The number of Cantonese immigrants to Latin America in the last century is second only perhaps to Italians and Spanish. There are "Chinese" restaurants in every Latin American city, but nowhere more than in Perú, where the term *chaufa*, transliterated from the Cantonese *chowfun* (or *zhaofen* in Pinyin-Mandarin), retains both its literal meaning (fried rice) and its general usage (greasy, no-frills takeout).

all-you-can-eat tacos.
taquiza libre.
In modern Mexico, tacos aren't restaurant food, they're practical, informal food—you get them at bars, but more often you get them on the street, in the parking lot of a sporting event, or at a market stall built from two milk crates. The term *taquiza* refers to "taco service"—as in, you contract the cart to serve your guests at a party, and they bring a portable kitchen and crank them out like a mobile factory. This is why Mexicans will sometimes tell you the only two words sweeter than "open bar" are *taquiza libre*.

suckling pig.
lechón.
It may seem like an odd form of street food, but there are places in Andean South America where carts wander the winter streets selling roasted, stuffed suckling pigs in little paper cups or plates. And if you've ever forgotten your overcoat on a long walk home from work in those regions, it stops sounding so gross after a couple blocks.

boneless, shell-less paella.
paella ciega.
Want Spain's signature complex rice dish but can't be bothered to pick rabbit bones and clam shells out of your lunch? Just order it *ciega*—ostensibly, they made it that way for blind people, but nowadays, lazy people are reaping the benefits. If you're at a real fancy place, you can even tell them how to cook it: soupy (*caldoso*), al dente (*meloso*), or crunchy (*soccorat* or *socorrado*).

I'm full.
Estoy lleno/a.

I'm stuffed.
Estoy repleto/a.

I'm gonna burst!
¡Estoy quebrado/a!

Yum-yum!
¡Ñam-ñam!

It's really good!
¡Está buenísimo!

That was…
Eso era…

> **a good meal.**
> *una buena comida.*
>
> **really tasty.**
> *muy sabroso.*
>
> **delicious.**
> *delicioso.*
>
> **scrumptious.**
> *riquísimo.*

filling.
saciante.

Yuck!
¡Qué asco!

That's foul.
*¡Eso es **un asco**!*

Their food is crap.
Su comida es una mierda.

It's disgusting.
Es un asquete.

I think I just lost my appetite.
*Acabo de **perder el apetito**.*

I think you just cost me my appetite.
*Acabas de **quitarme el apetito**.*

A farmhand wouldn't eat that shit in the middle of a drought!
*¡Un peón **no comería esa mierda** en plena sequía!*

I'm not gonna eat…
No voy a comer…

> **this bullshit.**
> *esta bosta.*
> Literally, "manure."

> **this revolting garbage.**
> *esta basura inmunda.*

> **that abomination.**
> *esa abominación.*

> **this steaming turd.**
> *esta cagada humeante.*

Uhh…my stomach's really upset.
Uuu…me siento descompuesto.

I think those shrimp gave me indigestion.
*Me parece que esos camarones **se me indigestaron**.*

·····Drinks
Bebidas

I'm thirsty.
Tengo sed.

My throat is parched. Could you give me…?
Tengo la garganta seca. ¿Me darías…?

> **some tap water**
> *agua de canilla*
>
> **a sparkling water, no ice**
> *un agua con gas, natural*
>
> **very cold soda**
> *una soda bien fría*
>
> **a stupid-cold Coke**
> *una coca casi congelada*
>
> **a milk shake**
> *un licuado* (LatAm) | *un batido* (Spn)
>
> **a frappé**
> *un granizado*
>
> **a smoothie**
> *un licuado* | *batido de fruta* | *un biónico* (Mex)

·····Get your juice on
Sacarle el jugo

Latin Americans love fruit juice almost as much as they love rich, meaty food—if not for fruit juice, they would be sitting ducks for the foreign laxative industry. Here are some exotic potables to try in your travels:

> ### *Jugo de caña / Guarapo*
> Sugarcane is the basis for all kinds of drinks, most famously rum, its more primitive form *cachaça*, and its stronger distillation, *aguardiente de caña* (known to its friends as *caña, ron blanco, aguardient de guarapo*, "why your grandpa doesn't see so well" or "where your college fund went"). But did you know that you can actually drink straight sugarcane juice if it's fresh enough, and that it's not nearly as sweet as

COFFEE TOURISM)))
TURISMO CAFEINADO

Juan Valdéz jokes aside (and please, let's keep them aside; growing up a Juan in America you hear them all), coffee really is essential to the lifestyle and economy of much of the Spanish-speaking world. Nowadays, the trend in America is toward $5 artisanal masterpieces, but for a hundred years most Latin Americans have paid well under $1 a cup for their morning fix and afternoon pick-me-up, allowing marathon workdays and all-night parties unheard of in the business-minded North. Maybe that's why the *siesta* is rapidly going extinct.

In the Caribbean, coffee is made in 2- to 8-shot stovetop aluminum espresso kettles called *cafetines*. In South America, hourglass-shaped drippers called *milettas* make pragmatic coffee in extended-family pots, while urban elites sip individual shots (*café cortos*), micro lattes (*cortados*), and French-style mega lattes (*café con leche*) of espresso made in Italian machines. In Spain, as well as most of Latin America except Colombia and coffee-producing regions of Perú, it's hard to find coffee that hasn't been *torrado*, or roasted in oil sweetened with raw sugarcane that kind of caramelizes onto the bean, creating a sugary-smoky overtone that some people find delicious and others worry might be cancerous. Mexicans have come up with their own country-style variation on this roasting process, and many grandmothers and old-fashioned restaurants offer their guests *café de olla*. It's usually drip-filtered on the weak side, and adding milk is strictly taboo.

In most Latin American countries you can order an espresso "long" or "short" (*largo* or *corto*), but in Spain a single shot is a *café solo*, and a double is a *café doble*. In Spain, asking for a *café con hielo* will get you a small cup packed tightly with ice and an espresso shot for you to splash on at the last minute. In Latin America, you're much more likely to get presweetened iced coffee American-style.

Every coffee lover should go to Colombia at least once in their life: Starbucks-style mega-chains compete nationwide for the urban takeout market with new flavored syrups and slushy machines that you'd only see at a 7-Eleven in the U.S. Meanwhile, tony boutiques vie for the high-end crowd, serving espressos lovingly pulled by hand while explaining to you the names of every hill and valley where each bean was hand-picked by an organic farmer they know called Luís.

you'd expect? When you're in a city in a sugar-producing country, listen for the sound of repurposed lawn mower engines and follow them to street vendors pulling sugarcanes out of giant bundles to fill tiny Dixie cups for a coin or two. Best with a touch of lemon.

Aguapanela

Another tooth-rotting beverage is Colombia's *aguapanela*, which is made by dissolving a brick of sugarcane (called a *panela*, *piloncillo* [Mex], *chancaca* [Per], panocha, etc.) in boiling water with a little lemon juice. Not your cup of tea? Then maybe you should go to the other end of the spectrum, like…

Zumo de amargo

In Seville, they grow some of the best citrus in the world—and also some of the most bitter, like the *naranjo amargo*, an orange so bitter that, aside from its use in Italian digestive bitters and pork marinades, is too bitter for the rest of the world to even consider as a breakfast option. Bottoms up!

Jugo de cajú (pronounced, kah-JOO) | Jugo de merey (Ven) | Jugo de cajuil (DoR) | Jugo de maranon (Carib)

Native to Brazil but cultivated in Venezuela and other Caribbean countries, the cashew nut is actually tiny in comparison to the fruit it grows attached to—but 94 percent of the cashew fruits grown commercially are thrown away after removing the prized nut. The other 6 percent are mostly used to make vinegar or to make an incredibly tart juice that takes a good bit of sugar to be palatable—luckily sugar usually grows cheaply nearby.

Vampiro

This classic Mexico City fruit blend is far removed from the palette most people stereotypically associate with Mexican cuisine. The name comes from the blood-red color imparted by raw beets, and celery brings a strong savory overtone that usually overpowers even the orange or pineapple juice. It is, however, the breakfast of choice for most *chilangos* (Distrito Federal natives)—it's just the thing to get you back to work after a heavy, spicy dinner and a tequila nightcap.

·····At the restaurant
En el restaurante

Service in the Spanish-speaking world isn't *bad*—it just doesn't give a shit about you. That's because there's no incentive, since tips in most of Latin America range from whatever coins come back in your change to a whopping 10 percent. It's not even that rude to leave no tip if you're short that week. But tip or no tip, the waitstaff won't "wait" on you: They do their own thing until you call, and if they don't like how you call them over, they play deaf, look busy, or pick up the phone to call their girlfriend.

Bring me…
Traígame…

> **the menu. (more formal)**
> *la carta.*

> **the menu. (less formal)**
> *el menú.*
> In much of South America, the lunch or dinner special is also called *el menú.*

> **the check.**
> *la cuenta.*

> **a bread basket.**
> *una canasta de pan.*

> **some steamed tortillas.**
> *algunas tortillas al vapor.*

> **the silverware.**
> *los cubiertos.*

Can we **order**?
*¿Podemos **pedir**?*

What would you recommend to a first-timer?
*¿**Qué recomendarías** a un principiante?*

Tell me, does *cuy* mean **guinea pig**?
*Dime, ¿cuy quiere decir **conejo de indias**?*

THERE'S A WORM IN MY TEQUILA. CALL...)))
HAY UN GUSANO EN MI TEQUILA. LLÁMAME...

the manager
el gerente

your boss
tu jefe

the chef
el chef
If they actually pronounce it in proper French, you're probably paying too much for your food.

the cook
el cocinero

the waiter /waitress
el camarero/a

the dimwit that took my order
el/la lelo/a que me tomó el orden

the wine steward
el/la sommelier
It's French, and he probably is, too; you're not at a place serving local specialties.

the barbecue master
el/la asador/a
This is a proud profession and a guarded position in most of Latin America. The BBQ master ranks even higher than the chef in most kitchens.

Five bucks if you can **name every organ** in my bowl of menudo.
*Cincuenta pesos si me puedes **nombrar cada órgano** en mi plato de menudo.*

What's taking so long? **Did they head out to the farm** to find my chicken, or what?
*¿Qué demora tanto? ¿**Se fueron al rancho** para elegir la gallina, o qué?*

Should we leave a tip?
¿Debemos dejar una propina?

I don't have any dough on me, but I could do the dishes to settle up.
No tengo nada de billullo conmigo, pero podría lavar los platos para ajustar la cuenta.

•••••Mystery meats
Carnes ocultas

Much to the chagrin of Texas, "barbecue" isn't even an English word. *Barbacoa* was an old Latin American custom brought across the Rio Grande by Mexican cowherds, who, along with their counterparts in Spain and South America, had been getting their grill on for centuries. And after all that time heating their meat, they've come up with some pretty, um, "interesting" things to grill. I raise my fork to you, daring *asadores*!

Grill me up some...
Tírame un poco de...en la parrilla.

How much protein is there in...?
¿Cuánta proteina hay en el...?

I'm on a strict diet of...
Estoy a dieta estricta de...

Chicharrón
Deep-fried strips of pork skin or thicker cuts

Molleja
Sweetbreads (i.e., the thymus gland of a young lamb or calf). It's pretty safe to eat these in Latin America (especially in Argentina and Uruguay) where ranchers often exceed organic standards.

Butifarra
A peppery pork sausage. The white variety is made entirely of lean pork, while the black kind is packed with pork fat and blood.

Morcilla
Coagulated blood sausage. Consider yourself warned.

Garrobo
A kind of iguana, usually served in a broth.

Callos
A Spanish form of tripe (i.e., beef stomach) from a younger, less world-weary digestive tract. Mmmm!

Chinchulines
Chunks of barbecued intestine. You may wanna check that they've been completely emptied.

Cuy
Guinea pig. In rural parts of the Andes, you'll find street vendors selling whole roasted guinea pigs out of their carts like hot dogs.

·····Street food
Comida callejera

Spanish speakers don't go in for fast food the way Americans do. Why deal with fluorescent lights, ugly uniforms, and zit-faced teens when you can buy cheaper food from a grizzled, one-eyed mountain man pushing a griddle around in a shopping cart? The food just tastes better that way.

I'm dying for a good…
Estoy muriendo por un buen…

Taco (Mexico)

Think you know something about tacos just cuz you can say *carne asada*? You don't know shit. Not until you've tried tacos *al pastor* (spicy, spit-roasted pork), *tacos árabes* (in pita bread), tacos stuffed with spicy *papas* (bright-red mashed potatoes), *nopales* (cactus), *buche* (tripe), *ubre* (udder), *cuerno* (horn-skinflap), *bofe* (lung), *suadero* (bacon with the skin left on), *trompa* (lips), and *sesos* (brains). Makes your local *taquería* seem a little less authentic, no?

Huarache (Southern Mexico)

This Aztec forerunner of the modern taco is made thick from fresh yellow or blue corn, shaped like the sole of a sandal (hence the name), stuffed with a layer of black beans, and traditionally topped with cheese, *salsa verde*, sautéed mushrooms, and/or squash flowers.

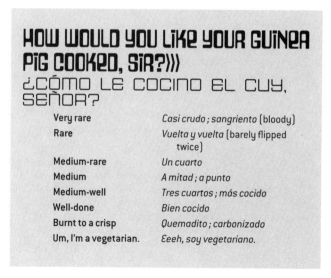

HOW WOULD YOU LIKE YOUR GUINEA PIG COOKED, SIR?)))
¿CÓMO LE COCINO EL CUY, SEÑOR?

Very rare	*Casi crudo; sangriento* (bloody)
Rare	*Vuelta y vuelta* (barely flipped twice)
Medium-rare	*Un cuarto*
Medium	*A mitad; a punto*
Medium-well	*Tres cuartos; más cocido*
Well-done	*Bien cocido*
Burnt to a crisp	*Quemadito; carbonizado*
Um, I'm a vegetarian.	*Eeeh, soy vegetariano.*

Pupusa (Honduras, Guatemala, El Salvador)

This handmade griddle-cake is like a *huarache* but bigger and perfectly round, often filled with *queso y loroco* (the sweet bud of a native vine), *queso y chipilín* (a savory herb), or *revueltas* (a combination of cheese, *chicharrón*, and sometimes refried beans). A good *pupusa* will fill you up like nobody's business.

Elote (Central America)

The name *elote* refers specifically to sweet corn. When an *elotero* yells the word on the street, though, they're talkin' 'bout corn on the cob, boiled, roasted, or barbecued on a jerry-rigged shopping cart. Spice it up with room-temperature mayo, *cotija* cheese, *chilitos*, lime juice, salt, and *Tequesquite* (a pre-Columbian mineral salt).

Tamal (Central America, Andes)

The further south you go, the weirder tamales get. Banana leaf-steamed *tamales yucatecas* are stuffed with pork marrow, annatto seed, and sour orange stew. *Tamales pishques* have refried beans and ash stirred in with the cornmeal masa. The huge, intense Nicaraguan *nacatamal* has annatto-seed pork, rice, potatoes, mint, olives, and raisins. Some Andean tamales include peanuts, turtle meat, and African herbs, while in Northern Argentina the *masa* is half corn and half squash.

Atol (Central America)

The name *atol* refers to both chowdery soups and hot drinks, often sold out of giant soup thermoses pushed around in a baby stroller. The most common Mexican *atol* is *achampurrado*, a thick, modern form of Aztec hot cocoa (with cinnamon, chile pepper, and whole milk). In many countries you'll get a bowl of savory, bean-watery *atoles* when you buy *pupusas*, whether from a restaurant, a window counter, or some guy with an eye-patch pushing a cart down the street.

Aguafresca (Central America)

These cooling, sugary beverages come in an infinite array of flavors, including hibiscus blossom, mango, watermelon, tamarind, sugarcane, and papaya. You can even still find some of the pre-Columbian *aguasfrescas* like *tepache* (fermented pineapple rind and crude cane), *pinole* (sweet spices and roasted cornmeal), *lechuguilla* (a kind of agave cactus), and *tesgüino* (a malty corn beer). Go for it, young adventurer!

THE NOT-SO-UNIVERSAL LANGUAGE OF GRUB)))

GRUB	TO GRUB/CHOW DOWN
El refín (Mex)	*Refinar* | *echar papa* (Mex)
El pipirín | *el merol* (CenAm)	*Jamar* (CenAm)
El papeo | *la jala* (Spn)	*Jalar; jamar* | *papear* (Spn)
La manya (S.Cone)	*Morfar* | *manyar* (S.Cone)
La jama (Andes)	*Jamear* | *combear* | *papear* (Andes)
La jama | *el pasto* (Carib)	*Jamar* (Carib)

Migas, aka *migas de pastor* (Southern Spain)

This couscouslike dish was traditionally made from hard bread and was cooked in a big pan with bacon or pigskin and a bunch of other meats, veggies, and even sweets like melon, grapes, or chocolate. It's not much to look at when the vendor is stirring it around with a big wooden stick, but trust me, it's legit.

Ceviche (Perú, Ecuador, Mexico)

Perú is proud of its only major culinary export—few people outside Japan get this excited about raw fish. Ceviche is "cooked" by adding acidic vinegar and lime juice that kill more microbes than most "real" cooking. There are tons of regional variations, like the shellfish- and sea snail–heavy Ecuadorian kind, or the uncannily black *conchas negras* ceviche served in a shell with *plátanos* or *batata* and toasted corn.

Paella (Spain)

This famous rice dish is named after the pan it's cooked in, a huge, shallow vat that evaporates moisture out quickly. The most famous paella, the saffron-laden Valencian kind, takes all day to cook and incorporates as many sea snails and shellfish as the season allows. *Paella mixta* "mixes in" rabbit and chicken with the shellfish. And *arroz negro* is a *paella* dyed black with squid or cuttlefish ink, great for adventurous eaters and cephalopod buffs alike.

Bacalao al pil-pil (Northwestern Spain)

This freaky Basque dish involves slow-cooking big chunks of cod, garlic, and tiny chili peppers in tons of olive oil until the oil congeals into a gelatinous sauce. Basque doesn't have a word for the texture, which is probably why they made up the onomatopoetic *pil-pil*. Or maybe someone just tried to trick their kids into eating it by giving it a cute name, 'cuz it's pretty damn gross.

Plátanos, aka *tajadas* (Caribbean, Central America)

Fried plantains cut in strips (*tajadas*) to maximize the frying area *and* your cholesterol. Beware of *patacón pisao*: nasty, deep-fried green plantain peel. *Tostones*, on the other hand, are delicious since they're mashed halfway through cooking to get a nice, varied texture.

·····Other grub
Otras manducas

Let's face it, Spanish speakers are Catholics, and Catholics have a lot of mouths to feed. And there's no more efficient way to use all the scraps in the fridge than to throw together a sandwich, make a stew, or stuff last night's leftovers into some dough and bake it in the oven.

Go make me a...sandwich.
Anda a hacerme un sandwich...

Cubano (Caribbean)
The porkiest sandwich on earth! To make an old-school *cubano*, you take a roll shortened with pig-lard, warm it in pig-lard on a griddle, and add swiss cheese, ham, and roast pork.

De miga (Argentina, Uruguay)
A crustless sandwich made from paper-thin slices of white bread, heavy on the mayo. The traditional fillings are ham, processed cheese, slices of oily pepper and/or palm hearts, lettuce, tomato, and an olivey egg salad. Throw one into a panini grill and you have the best snack every invented, known simply as *un tostado*.

De jamón serrano, aka *jamón curado* (Spain)

The ham in these sandwiches is dried and salt-cured for one to two years in whole hocks that often hang over the counter in a bar or deli. The prized *ibérico* variety is cured longer and made from pigs raised on a diet of grass and acorns (*bellotas*). Pair this with some dry cheese and you're in business.

Pambazo (Guadalajara)

This gut-busting local variation on the Mexican *torta* (a lighter "Cuban" with avocado, raw onion, and beans) ups the heartburn ante with peppery *chorizo*, hot sauce, and bright-red mashed potatoes.

Let's stew up some...
Pongámonos a guisar un/una...

Locro (Argentina, Bolivia, Paraguay)

A thick-as-peanut-butter stew featuring hominy, beans, and often tendony shredded meat scraps. When done right, it's amazing.

Ropa vieja (Cuba)

Fancy shredded pork stewed in a tomato-based *criollo* sauce, with the texture of the tattered rags your mom makes you throw out, hence the name "old clothes."

Menudo (Mexico)

Most of the organs in this stew (including the free-floating eyeballs in some recipes) retain their shape and appear whole in your bowl.

Mondongo (Local variations in every country in Latin America)

Tripe-heavy haggis with yucca, cornmeal cakes, and exotic purple potatoes.

Posole aka *pozol* (Southern Mexico, Honduras, Guatemala)

A pork stew with hominy and pig organs slow-cooked in a chile-chicken broth. At the last minute, you dump in tons of fresh oregano, lime juice, and onion. The guest of honor gets a big piece of pig's face in their bowl, and everyone else who gets a foot gets good luck (or something).

YOU SAY TOMATO, i SAY JÍTOMATE)))

Throughout Latin America, particularly where each indigenous language is native, many fruits and veggies are still called by their pre-Columbian names instead of their standard Spanish ones.

Tomato (the big, firm kind)	*Jítomate* (Nahuatl)
Peanut	*Maní* (Taino)
Chili pepper	*Ají* (Taino)
Squash	*Ayote* (Nahuatl), *Pipián* (Mayan), *Zapallo* (Quechua)
Sweet potato	*Camote* (Nahuatl), *Boniato* (Taino)
Corn	*Elote* (Nahuatl), *Choclo* (Quechua)
Avocado	*Aguacate* (Nahuatl), *Palta* (Quechua)

Chupe (Bolivia, Perú, Colombia, Paraguay, Chile, Panamá)
This is a general term for various buttery, white soups, made with barley, corn, or other grains, plus enough big chunks of meat that you'll need a knife to go along with your spork.

Olla podrida (Western Spain)
The name of the dish literally means, "putrid pot" (and boy, am I hungry now!). It's a rich red-bean stew thickened with bacon, blood sausage, and smoked pig's ear, rib, and snout. Nothing says delicious like pig snout.

Your mom sure knows how to bake a mean...
Sí que tu vieja sabe hornear una buena...

Sope, aka **pellizcada**, **picadita** (Mexico)
This is like a taco-pizza—almost twice as large as a taco, thicker (and still soft and gooey inside), turned up at the edges like a pizza crust, and topped evenly instead of mounded like a taco.

Gordita (Mexico)

Imagine a hot-pocket made by flash-frying a stuffed hand-made tortilla, then cutting it in half and stuffing in cheese while it's still hot enough to melt it, then baking it to a crisp.

Empanada (Southern Cone, Colombia)

The Argentine variety is best described as a hand-held calzone. They're usually filled with ham and cheese, spiced meat, spinach, or *humita* (a sweet corn white sauce). Chilean ones are more like flakey meat turnovers, and Colombian ones are like English potpies, usually fried instead of baked. Central Americans use the term for any number of baked things, from oven-quesadillas to pies to casseroles.

I've got a bit of a sweet tooth. I could really go for some/a…

Soy medio goloso. Estoy antojando…

Helado de mamey

When you're in tropical regions, a healthy distrust of local dairy products is both logical and recommended: As a seasoned backpacker once told me, "Don't eat ice cream anywhere refrigeration costs more than health care." One exception I recommend making to this axiom is for ice cream made with the Caribbean's weirdest, pulpiest fruit, the *mamey*. Other exotic pulpy fruit flavors to try: South American *guanabana* (aka "soursop"), the smaller Mexican *chirimoya*, Peruvian *lúcuma* (even pastier!), and local varieties of *higo* (fig).

Horchata

The only ingredient that the various Spanish, Mexican, and Andean varieties of this sweet dessert and/or beverage share is water and rice flour of some kind—beyond that, you really don't know what you're ordering until you drink it. Walnuts (Oaxaca) and almonds (Andalucía) might be floating in it; it might be disgustingly sweet or refreshingly watery or kind of savory; it might have cinnamon, cloves, nutmeg, allspice, or even artificial cinnamon syrup (i.e., liquid Red Hots); it might be piping hot, lukewarm, or full of ice.

Crema catalana

Don't let a proud Cataluñian hear you call it crème brûlée—they're pretty confident that they invented it and that the French ripped them off.

Manjar blanco

This debatably pre-Colombian Peruvian treat is best described as a dense, layered combination of toffee, milk caramel and shortbread. There are regional variations all over the country (many using exotic caramels made from the milk of goats, sheep, or even llamas), but any way you slice it, your dentist doesn't want you eating it!

Alfajores

Across the Spanish-speaking world, there are boatloads of dry, crumbly cookies and biscuits that share this (notably Arabic) name, but Argentineans have elevated it to the level of a national specialty. The typical Argentine versions consist of a huge gob of *dulce de leche* (rich milk caramel) or, in some cases, regional fruit jam between two cookies or sconelike biscuits. Since the nineteenth century, chocolate-coated, coconut-dusted, and/or meringue-covered variations have been competing in a Cold War of regional specialties and niche markets; a group of alfanerds in Buenos Aires even run a blog rating the hundreds of licensed manufacturers nationwide.

Agarapiñadas (Spn, S.Cone) | Garapiñado (Mex)

When you think "Spanish peanuts," you probably think of those disgusting packaged sugar-coated peanuts you get at truck stops when you're too drunk or stoned to reason clearly about your snacking options. Those pathetic American nut bags are in fact descended from a noble line of caramelized nuts (usually peanuts, but sometimes almonds, walnuts, hazelnuts, or a combination), which are traditionally sold in street carts or, in rare cases, packaged and served cold. The secret ingredient is baking soda, which makes the caramel bubble and blister as it heats—only to cool rapidly into that satisfying, brittle texture.

[Pastel de] Tres Leches

No one knows exactly where the *tres leches* comes from, but in all its variations, this cream-based pastry has a distinctly airy texture and about as much saturated fat per serving as is humanly possible without butter or lard. It's kind of like a 1950s tiramisu, except sweeter. The name refers to three forms of dairy you combine with flour before baking: canned evaporated milk, canned condensed milk and either heavy whipping cream (Mex, Spn) or coconut cream (Carib). As if that weren't enough action, hot-rodding Spanish speakers soup up the damn thing with additional "creams": whipped cream topping and sweetened rum or brandy get thrown on top to make it a full-blown *pastel borracho*.

Mazamorra

Although this pre-Colombian method for milling cornmeal survives in many forms, the most famous is Perú's bright-purple corn pudding, sweetened with cane sugar and dyed naturally by a kind of local, high-elevation corn that produces even stronger purple hues than beets do. Some of the more savory variations got Paraguay through the six-year food shortage of the Three Alliances war, while an *horchata*-like beverage by the same name accompanies the typical dish of the Colombian highlanders, the *bandeja paisa*.

Churros

Although the longer, cinnamon-heavy variety has been a staple of Mexican county fairs and Mexican-American restaurants, even the proudest Mexican will usually acknowledge that the original churros are short, unspiced *churros madrileños*. What's harder is getting a Spaniard to acknowledge the resemblance between churros and similar-looking North African fried desserts. Whatever the case, a few churros dipped in hot cocoa are just the thing to get through a winter night—or to soak up that ninth whiskey while you wait for the trains to start running again.

·····Other Ulysses Press Titles

Dirty Chinese: Everyday Slang from "What's Up?" to "F*%# Off!"

MATT COLEMAN & EDMUND BACKHOUSE, **$10.00**

Dirty Chinese features phrases for every situation, even expressions to convince a local official that you have waited long enough and tipped him plenty already. A pronunciation guide, a reference dictionary and sample dialogues make this guide invaluable for those traveling to China.

Dirty Czech: Everyday Slang from "What's Up?" to "F*%# Off!"

MARTIN BLAHA, **$10.00**

Nothing is censored in *Dirty Czech*. There are enough insults and swear words to offend every person in the Czech Republic—without even mentioning that Slovakia plays better ice hockey—and sweet words to entice a local beauty to stroll along Prague's Vltava River.

Dirty French: Everyday Slang from "What's Up?" to "F*%# Off!"

ADRIEN CLAUTRIER & HENRY ROWE, **$10.00**

With enough insults and swear words to offend every person in France without even speaking to them in English (which they really dislike), *Dirty French* has phrases for every situation, including expressions for describing art that make one sound smart and cool.

Dirty German: Everyday Slang from "What's Up?" to "F*%# Off!"

DANIEL CHAFFEY, **$10.00**

Dirty German provides enough insults to offend every person in Germany—without even mentioning that the Japanese make better cars—as well as explicit sex terms that'll even embarrass the women of Hamburg's infamous red light district.

Dirty Korean: Everyday Slang from "What's Up?" to "F*%# Off!"

HAEWON GEEBI BAEK, **$10.00**

Dirty Korean presents cool things to say for all casual situations, including harsh expressions to convince a local police officer that one's documents are in order and he has been tipped enough, sweet words to entice a local beauty to join you for a plate of kimchi, and even native banter to help make friends over a glass of *soju*.

Dirty Portuguese: Everyday Slang from "What's Up?" to "F*%# Off!"

ALICE ROSE, NATI VALE & PEDRO A. CABRAL, **$10.00**

No one speaks in strictly formal address anymore, especially in Brazil, where the common expressions tossed around in their party-friendly cities are far from textbook Portuguese. This totally-up-to-date book fills the gap between how people really talk in Brazil and what Portuguese-language students are taught.

Dirty Russian: Everyday Slang from "What's Up?" to "F*%# Off!"

ERIN COYNE & IGOR FISUN, **$10.00**

An invaluable guide for off-the-beaten-path travelers going to Russia, *Dirty Russian* is packed with enough insults and swear words to offend every person in Russia without even mentioning that they lost the Cold War.

To order these books call 800-377-2542 or 510-601-8301, fax 510-601-8307, e-mail ulysses@ulyssespress.com, or write to Ulysses Press, P.O. Box 3440, Berkeley, CA 94703. All retail orders are shipped free of charge. California residents must include sales tax. Allow two to three weeks for delivery.